I0805430

"I read *Blessed Is the Body* with an ache in my chest. Like so many others, I grew up under a religious narrative that equated my visibly disabled body with sin. Tatum Tricarico powerfully disrupts a harmful framework and offers a much-needed counternarrative. Sitting with her reflections on disability justice and Christian theology is tending to parts of a wound I'm still trying to understand."

REBEKAH TAUSSIG, author of *Sitting Pretty: The View from My Ordinary Resilient Disabled Body*

"Pondering disability justice as the body of Christ through a Lenten devotional is as brilliant as it is impactful, and as challenging as it is profoundly encouraging. Tatum Tricarico is a skillful guide, teaching us all the numerous ways that the image of God shows up in the diversity of humanity right in front of us."

BENJAMIN CREMER, pastor, author, and creator of *Into the Gray* newsletter and podcast

"In *Blessed Is the Body*, Tatum Tricarico's unflinching honesty gives rise to freedom, inviting us to embrace the truth that our human bodies—finite, disabled, ever-changing—are how God created us and where God delights to dwell. The thoughtful reflection questions and multisensory practices that accompany each day's devotional make this book beautifully accessible for people who learn and connect with God in different ways. A Lenten journey well worth taking."

BETHANY MCKINNEY FOX, pastor and author of *Disability and the Way of Jesus: Holistic Healing in the Gospels and the Church*

"*Blessed Is the Body* breaks new ground in theology and disability literature by combining individual stories, disability justice history in America, biblical studies, and pastoral and community care into a joyful and sobering series of Lenten daily devotionals. Tatum Tricarico thus breaks disability out of specialized interpretive boxes and illuminates the spiritual and theological issues at the heart of living a faithful and flourishing life along with disability, not in spite of it."

BILL GAVENTA, author of *Spirituality and Disability: Recovering Wholeness* and speaker, trainer, and consultant primarily in the arena of faith and disability

"*Blessed Is the Body* draws from the wells of Christian Scripture and Disability experience to affirm the realities of human finitude, beauty, and interdependence. Tatum Tricarico welcomes both disabled and nondisabled readers into Lenten practices of embodied prayer, reflection, and connection. By enlivening our prayers, challenging our assumptions, and empowering our actions, this devotional companions us into a future marked by disability justice.

SARAH JEAN BARTON, assistant professor at Duke Divinity School and author of *Becoming the Baptized Body: Disability and the Practice of Christian Community*

BLESSED
IS THE
BODY

BLESSED IS THE BODY

DISABILITY JUSTICE AND THE COMMUNITY OF CHRIST

TATUM TRICARICO

A LENTEN DEVOTIONAL

HERALD PRESS
Harrisonburg, Virginia

Herald Press
PO Box 866, Harrisonburg, Virginia 22803
www.HeraldPress.com

Library of Congress Cataloging-in-Publication Data
Names: Tricarico, Tatum author
Title: Blessed is the body : disability justice and the community of Christ : (a lenten devotional) / Tatum Tricarico.
Description: Harrisonburg, Virginia : Herald Press, [2025] | Includes bibliographical references.
Identifiers: LCCN 2025015110 (print) | LCCN 2025015111 (ebook) | ISBN 9781513815459 paperback | ISBN 9781513815466 ebook
Subjects: LCSH: People with disabilities--Prayers and devotions | Lent--Prayers and devotions | BISAC: RELIGION / Holidays / Easter & Lent | RELIGION / Christian Living / Social Issues | LCGFT: Devotional literature | Prayers
Classification: LCC BV4460 .T75 2025 (print) | LCC BV4460 (ebook) | DDC 259/.4--dc23/eng/20250828
LC record available at https://lccn.loc.gov/2025015110
LC ebook record available at https://lccn.loc.gov/2025015111

Study guides are available for many Herald Press titles at www.HeraldPress.com.

BLESSED IS THE BODY

Library of Congress Control Number: 2025015110
International Standard Book Number: 978-1-5138-1545-9 (paperback); 978-1-5138-1546-6 (ebook)
Printed in United States of America
Cover: anfisa_focusova / iStock / Getty Images Plus; Sofia Junkhaw / iStock / Getty Images Plus; LeMusique / iStock / Getty Images Plus

29 28 27 26 25 10 9 8 7 6 5 4 3 2 1

For Judy Heumann, Lois Curtis, Ed Roberts, Zona Roberts, Stacey Park Milbern, HolLynn D'Lil, and Neil Jacobson, the Disabled leaders, mentors, activists, and friends who became my ancestors as I learned about my own Disabled identity. You lived your lives in a way that allowed me more access to mine, and I promise to continue in your legacy.

Contents

WEEK 4: CONNECTED

WEEK 5: HEALED

WEEK 6: ANOINTED

Introduction

One of my good friends in fourth grade stuttered. Every time she was asked to read aloud, I would pray silently, "God, help her not to stutter," because I hated how the kids would laugh. But now, if I were sitting there today, I'd change my prayer. I'd pray, "God, let them listen," because the stuttering is not the problem, the laughter is.

Now, I often stand in front of people, reading from a Braille script or repeating from a headphone playing the script in my ear. Yearly, I stand in sanctuaries leading a program I've written that centers Disability Justice in the context of the Stations of the Cross. The Stations of the Cross come from the Catholic tradition and typically involve a series of images, or stations, focused on Jesus' journey to the cross. The program I wrote honors Jesus' crucifixion and its connection to the Disabled community.

At each church, I request that the pastor reach out to three other Disabled church members who would be interested in leading with me, or I bring my own friends. Disabled leadership is one of my favorite experiences, especially as I notice the diversity of voices, sounds, bodies, and movement even just among the four leaders as we make our way around the sanctuary, speaking at each station. People have read the script with someone whispering in their ear when they can't read. They've read with stuttering voices or voices that are quieter or louder than expected. They've read with AAC (augmentative and alternative communication—in this case, a computer speaking for them). They've had canes and wheelchairs and guide dogs. They've made repetitive motions like hand flapping or twirling hair with the props or their hands, known as stimming, which can help a person self-regulate. Or they've been invisibly Disabled.

The church members may start out praying like I did—"God, please help them do it differently"—but by the end, it's clear that Disabled leadership isn't less than. Disabled leadership helps us all to recognize the multitude of ways that God's image shows up. Every year during Lent at these events, we share about the connection between God and Disability, and each time, the Disabled leadership shows God's image and work. It shows the holiness of inclusion and acceptance. It shows the ways that God can call Disabled folks and love us for all of who we are. I pray that this devotional does just that. I pray, "God, let them listen, and read, and see, and sense you through the work of Disabled leadership in these pages."

Lent is a time of prayerful reflection on finitude. It is where we understand that we are finite bodies with a finite ability to do good. We are human, and that is a beautiful and honest declaration. But this also reminds us that we will not live forever. That we will never be able to do everything that we want to, even and especially when what we want to do is love our neighbor well. During Lent, the church calendar gives us a space to be honest and lament the ways that our bodies and our actions are not all that we want them to be.

While many of us are used to Christian spaces that say these realities of finitude mean that humanity is broken or lost, this book claims something different. Lent is not a time when we should feel condemned or guilty beyond help. Instead, it is a time to pause and finally say what we've been trying to hide all year: I am human. I can't do it all. I have failed. I can't keep going at this pace forever. I need help.

The blessing, then, is that for centuries, the church has set apart forty days to answer those statements with the reply: That is expected. That is human. That is Lent. And still, God calls you beloved.

These are heavy truths to name here, and even heavier truths to accept deep within ourselves. That is why Lent does not end on Ash Wednesday or start right at Holy Week. We are given forty days to dive into these life-changing truths about who we are and who God is. These forty days are what we are about to embark on together. I pray that they bring honesty, lament, healing, and peace to each of us in whatever ways we need.

I know that it is daunting to engage in lament and honesty about our bodies, lives, and all the moments when they don't feel like they fit into a tidy little box marked "perfect" or "endless." That is where this devotional comes in, and why it is unlike any other. Over the next several weeks, we will consider themes of Disability Justice and Lent in ways that I pray will allow you to read and connect with Scripture, reflect on and learn about Disability culture, and participate in full-body practices that help you internalize the depth of feelings that Lent and Disability Justice can bring up in us.

For Disabled people, it is often impossible to ignore the realities of finitude. Every day, we encounter ableist, discriminatory practices that remind us of our finitude. Ableism is the discrimination and prejudice against Disabled people.[1] Ableist beliefs and actions become a constant limiting of our bodies, minds, experiences, and connections to others. Alongside ableism, Disabled people may also face the very real limits of bodily pain, fatigue, and overstimulation, which are not inherently negative in the way that ableism is, but are still consistently pressing limits upon us.

Everything from being denied entrance to a restaurant to experiencing chronic pain shows us that limits are real—both those that our bodies hold us to and those that are forced upon us by other people. Because of those limits, Disabled people have a deeper connection with what it means to be finite, and we encounter God's love at the borders of those limits every day.

Before we dive further into theology, though, it's important for you to know a bit about me, your guide on this Lenten journey. I am a proud Disabled person, a Queer woman of faith, an extrovert, and someone who loves hosting dinner parties, playing board games, and writing letters. I am currently working at a church, and I recently graduated from divinity school on my way to become a pastor. In this devotional, I will share with you pieces of Disability Justice, history, and culture that have profoundly affected me. Throughout my life I have experienced varying levels of Blindness and Vision Impairment, as well as Chronic Illness. These identities and experiences have changed the way that I understand God.

In the weeks that follow, I offer glimpses of my story that will reveal to you more about who I am. My background in both Disability Justice and theology informs much of this book, and so do the other parts of who I am. More than my own experience, though, this book is formed by what I've found to be life-giving in the Disability Rights and Justice movements that have taken place throughout history and are growing even now. The language, story, and theology found in these pages come from a line of amazing Disabled activists who I have learned from and been changed by. Some of them I've had the opportunity to call mentor or friend.

You, reader or listener, play just as important of a role in this book as I do. You are also bringing the fullness of yourself to it. This book is for Disabled people, and it is for people who have never even heard the words *Disability* and *justice* in the same sentence. It is for people who have been practicing Lent since childhood, and for people who are fed up with the church. It is for you.

Each day of this devotional has four sections: read, reflect, consider, and connect. These include an excerpt from Scripture to read, a Disability Justice–based reflection on that text, questions to consider for yourself or as a group, and a way to connect throughout your day. Each Sunday of Lent provides a further opportunity to pause and pray. It is up to you how you engage with this book, but I pray that however you do it, you center what your body and mind need in this time. You can read this devotional alone or in a group. You can read a few days that seem interesting or come along for the entire journey. You can answer every question I pose in the "consider" sections and actively participate in every "connect" activity, or you can read them and move on. If one of the pieces is overwhelming or doesn't feel true to you, be free to take what you need and leave the rest. However you engage with this text, I hope that it expands the ways that you understand God, yourself, and the Disabled community.

Journeying through Lent with the perspective of Disability Justice lets us experience the power, connection, care, and joy that come with being honest about our finite bodies. Through this devotional, Lent and Disability will be woven together in a beautiful basket that will hold space for all of who we are—the beauty and the dust.

Week 1

Dust

JOHN 11:17–44

Ash Wednesday

Dust to Dust

READ

John 11:17–22: When Jesus arrived, he found that Lazarus had already been in the tomb four days. Now Bethany was near Jerusalem, some two miles away, and many of the Jews had come to Martha and Mary to console them about their brother. When Martha heard that Jesus was coming, she went and met him, while Mary stayed at home. Martha said to Jesus, "Lord, if you had been here, my brother would not have died. But even now I know that God will give you whatever you ask of him."

REFLECT

Many of us have a complicated relationship with Ash Wednesday. On Ash Wednesday, we face the fact that our bodies are finite and our goals of doing good and loving our neighbor sometimes fall apart. It may be difficult to acknowledge these realities, and holding the weight of them might feel far too heavy.

The wisdom of Ash Wednesday can be summarized in the line "Ashes to ashes, dust to dust," which is often the repeated phrase spoken over people as they receive a mark of ashes on their foreheads. This reminder of where our bodies start and end is a harsh truth that many people rarely reflect on throughout the year. That is why we are starting our Lenten journey at the point of death. Starting with the dust that Lazarus is actively returning to as he lies in the tomb.

Ash Wednesday is also a time when Christians accept our finitude and the limits of how we sin over and over, even when we try to love God and our neighbors well. This day allows us to remember two different limits. First, that our bodies and minds are limited, beautifully and honestly, by the truth of being human. And second, that we are limited, harmfully, by the sin that exists in the world.

Sadly, Ash Wednesday has become a day when some churches choose to link the finitude of people's bodies with the sins they have committed. While it is true that Ash Wednesday gives us an opportunity to reflect on the finitude of bodies and the finitude of our ability to do good, it is also true that these limits are not linked. We exist as finite bodies because that is who God created us to be, not because we haven't done enough good.

Many Disabled people know the hurt of how the church has linked sin and bodily limitations, but Jesus does not link them here or in other places in Scripture. Instead, Jesus honors both realities wholly and separately. Jesus mourns for his friend with Mary and Martha. He does not condemn them, saying that sin is a link to death or bodily limitation. Jesus cares for the bodies in his presence. He honors the pain that comes with finitude with the comfort of closeness of his own physical self. He listens to Martha's honest account of what her brother's finite body means to her in this heavy moment.

From a Disability perspective, Ash Wednesday holds space for both understanding bodily limits to be a reality, not something to be ashamed of, and understanding sin to be something that we cannot escape. Being embodied—that which is dust to dust—is not a failure, it is an honest reflection of who we are, who God has made us to be, and who Jesus became. As Jesus tends to Martha and the other mourners in this moment, shame is undone and care is found at the border of this bodily limitation. Jesus reaches into care and not condemnation.

Today, as we honor Ash Wednesday, let the ashes be a reminder that while sin is real and we do not always care and love in the ways that we should, we are cared for and loved by Jesus even still. Let the ashes also be a reminder that though our bodies will limit us to the point of pain and death, we are still worthy of receiving care and love even as we name the dust that we come from and return to.

CONSIDER

1. How have Ash Wednesday and Lent been presented to you in the past? Has this been harmful or helpful for your understanding of God? For your understanding of your own body and others' bodies?
2. Where do you feel the limits of your body? How can you honor those limits today instead of thinking of them as something to be ashamed of?

CONNECT

Find some dirt, dust, or ash. It could be dirt from your garden or a house plant, ashes from your church, or dust that you find beneath the bed. Hold it in your hand and remember, "ashes to ashes, dust to dust." Rub it into your hand and notice how it becomes part of you. Reflect on the limits that are part of your life now, both the beautiful limits that are a result of your body and the harmful limits imposed by sin from yourself or others.

Thursday

Of the Brightest Stardust

READ

John 11:23–27: Jesus said to her, "Your brother will rise again." Martha said to him, "I know that he will rise again in the resurrection on the last day." Jesus said to her, "I am the resurrection and the life. Those who believe in me, even though they die, will live, and everyone who lives and believes in me will never die. Do you believe this?" She said to him, "Yes, Lord, I believe that you are the Messiah, the Son of God, the one coming into the world."

REFLECT

A few years ago, I had an Ash Wednesday I will never forget. My grandmother had recently died and donated her body to science. After a few months of work with her body and brain, they told us they would cremate her and mail us the ashes. In what could only be a holy coincidence, her ashes were delivered to us on the morning of Ash Wednesday. Because of that, Ash Wednesday became more than just a day to put ashes on our foreheads and think about finitude. Now it is a day of remembrance and honoring of the ashes of a body that was once, and still is, so special to me. I remember seeing the box of ashes sitting on our kitchen table and thinking about the years when my grandmother would sit at that table on Christmas mornings and birthday dinners.

I called one of my wonderful philosophy professors to talk with her about what this timely delivery of ashes meant to my faith, and she reminded me of the importance of bodies, ashes, and dust. Yes, Ash Wednesday and Lent allow for a time of reflection on the dust that we were and will become. But it is also a time to examine how meaningful that dust really is at every point on its journey—from before my grandma was formed, to when she was sitting at our table on Christmas morning, to when her ashes sat on our table as we mourned. My professor reminded me that before any dust became people, it was stars that exploded, creating matter that would eventually become our bodies. We are made of stardust.

We are called, in this time of Lent, to understand the worth of dust, the worth of our bodies, the worth of our presence in the world. The Bible also tells us of the worth of dust in many different stories. From the start of creation, God tells us that we are created in the image of God and are very good. The dust was never worthless. We were never worthless. We were always created in God's image, always holding a piece of divinity in us, and always sprinkled with glimpses of stardust and God's presence.

Jesus is defined by Martha as "the Messiah, the Son of God, the one who has come into the world from God." The God described here is the God that became flesh, embracing the dust to be with us. Mary, Martha, and Lazarus meant enough to God that Jesus accompanied them on their journey and brought resurrection and life to the dust. Jesus brings resurrection and life, not just to Lazarus, but to all of humanity through the many encounters with God's presence that we have every day—moments where sisters and friends come together to mourn the loss of their brother, the joy of a grandmother's love on Christmas morning, or the conversations between a professor and her student trying to figure out the meaning of it all. We find the resurrection and the life that Jesus brings through all these moments of God's love. We find God through all these glimpses of stardust.

CONSIDER

1. In your life, when have you found glimpses of stardust, moments when God's love comes through people's bodies?
2. What areas of your life are you hoping that Jesus will bring resurrection and new life to?

CONNECT

Tonight, go outside and spend time under the stars. Remember the phrase, "Ashes to ashes, dust to dust." Think about the stars that exploded to make the dust that is us. Reflect on where you see stardust and God's love showing up in your life. You may even choose to make a wish on a star for Jesus to bring resurrection and new life to an area of your life.

Friday

Dust Worth Fighting For

READ

John 11:28–37: When [Martha] had said this, she went back and called her sister Mary and told her privately, "The Teacher is here and is calling for you." And when she heard it, she got up quickly and went to him. Now Jesus had not yet come to the village but was still at the place where Martha had met him. The Jews who were with her in the house consoling her saw Mary get up quickly and go out. They followed her because they thought that she was going to the tomb to weep there. When Mary came where Jesus was and saw him, she knelt at his feet and said to him, "Lord, if you had been here, my brother would not have died." When Jesus saw her weeping and the Jews who came with her also weeping, he was greatly disturbed in spirit and deeply moved. He said, "Where have you laid him?" They said to him, "Lord, come and see." Jesus began to weep. So the Jews said, "See how he loved him!" But some of them said, "Could not he who opened the eyes of the blind man have kept this man from dying?"

REFLECT

In today's scripture, Mary repeats Martha's words: "Lord, if you had been here, my brother would not have died." Jesus had wanted to see Mary, but when she gets there, she doesn't even give him time to speak. She repeats her sister's words that let Jesus know what they think should have happened.

It is beautiful that these sisters, who have already named Jesus as the Son of God, still take the space to tell him how they wish he would have done things differently. They recognize his power and love so much that they know that if he had come earlier, Lazarus would have lived. But they also trust and respect him enough to say what they were thinking and to advocate for what they wish would have happened for their brother. They face the power that they know could change things, and they advocate for better. They know how sacred Lazarus's life was, and they advocate with that in mind.

These women are an example of advocacy and allyship. They know what their brother needs and they name it—even in the face of a friend and even in the face of God. Allyship means to come alongside those on the margins and advocate with them, especially as someone who is not marginalized in the same way. This is core to the experience of both Disabled people and Christians. As Christians, we are called to love our neighbor, which often means advocating for what they need alongside them. Disabled people are both in need of allies and are some of the best allies I have ever found.

While all Disabled people have extremely different experiences, there is still beautiful solidarity among the community as we advocate for one another and allow non-Disabled people to advocate with us. While a Black Neurodivergent person has a very different experience from a White Queer Blind person, there is a call on each of them as Disabled community to advocate for each other. Non-Disabled people have this call to allyship as well.

Lent gives us space to recognize that we are finite, that we cannot do it all, and so allyship is a deeply Lenten practice, honoring the limits of those around us and coming alongside one another in community. Where one may falter, a community can thrive. We do this just as Mary and Martha did for Lazarus. In their story and in the story of Disabled community, allyship comes from a realization that people are sacred and deserving of love. The sacredness of Lazarus calls his sisters into the role of an ally. The sacredness of Disabled bodies and minds should call us all into allyship as well.

Jesus, in this text, clearly understands the sacredness of who Lazarus was too. Many of us know that the shortest verse in the Bible is "Jesus wept" (John 11:35 NIV). That statement means so much more in the context of Lazarus's life and the mourning of his sisters and friends. Jesus weeps because of his love for his friend. Jesus weeps because he knows life is finite, but also because he knows that Lazarus's life was sacred. This sacredness should make us weep for injustice and pain that others encounter. It should be the reason that we decide to be allies for our siblings, friends, and neighbors, no matter how different our experience is from theirs. So, I ask, how can we be like Mary and Martha? How can we recognize sacredness enough to face our friends and those in power and advocate for change?

CONSIDER

1. Think of a time someone was a good ally to you. What made their allyship meaningful?
2. What does it mean to think of Jesus in this allyship role? How does it feel to ask God to come alongside us, even for something scary or big?

CONNECT

Who in your life are you an ally to? Or, who in your life should you be a better ally to? Take a moment to send that person a message just to let them know that you're thinking of them and are in their corner. It could be anything from "Hey—just wanted to say I'm here for you" in a particular area of their life to a quick "Thinking of you" or "I've got your back." As you go about the next few days and weeks, follow through with your support and find ways that you could come alongside them well.

Saturday

Dusting Off Ideas of Disability

READ

John 11:38–44: Then Jesus, again greatly disturbed, came to the tomb. It was a cave, and a stone was lying against it. Jesus said, "Take away the stone." Martha, the sister of the dead man, said to him, "Lord, already there is a stench because he has been dead four days." Jesus said to her, "Did I not tell you that if you believed you would see the glory of God?" So they took away the stone. And Jesus looked upward and said, "Father, I thank you for having heard me. I knew that you always hear me, but I have said this for the sake of the crowd standing here, so that they may believe that you sent me." When he had said this, he cried with a loud voice, "Lazarus, come out!" The dead man came out, his hands and feet bound with strips of cloth and his face wrapped in a cloth. Jesus said to them, "Unbind him, and let him go."

REFLECT

My life changed when I became more noticeably Disabled. I had to learn a lot of new things. I had mobility specialists who taught me how to use my cane. I had TVIs (teachers of the Visually Impaired) who taught me to read Braille. I had neighbors, church members, and classmates who were Blind give me advice. I also found space on social media to learn from Disabled adults. They taught me everything from how to cook full meals on low "spoons" (energy) to tips on understanding relationships and sexuality as a Disabled person. There was so much to learn, and while some of it was scary, most of it was life-giving. It was finally honoring the truth of my body and accepting of all of who I was, especially when this learning came from one Disabled person to another.

Activist Stacey Park Milbern coined the term *crip doula* to describe these types of relationships. *Crip*, short for *crippled*, was previously used as an insult or negative metaphor. Now, though, the term has been reclaimed as a positive identity marker for the Disabled community, specifically when used by a Disabled person. A doula is someone who comes alongside a birth or death and accompanies the person with guidance and support. Milbern defines crip doulas as people who are "supporting people rebirthing themselves as Disabled or more Disabled."[2]

In today's scripture passage, Lazarus is coming into new life. His sisters and Jesus are there to "unbind him and let him go." This is a beautiful image of the three being doulas for Lazarus. This work does not just change his life, though. It changes all of them. Earlier, Martha had clearly been concerned about opening the tomb, and rightfully so, but I am sure that when the grave was opened, her concern turned quickly into a rush of other emotions that led her into new life as well. For both Martha and Lazarus, coming into new life meant leaving the grave and leaving behind their former belief of what was possible.

In my journey into Disability Justice, I had to do a lot of letting go, or dusting off, to bring new life as well. There were a few practical things I had to learn, specifically surrounding my identity and the language around it. I invite you to be changed by what I learned from my crip doulas as well.

First, I learned that *Disabled* is not a bad word. So many people use euphemisms like "special needs," "handi-capable," or "differently abled" to label us because the label of *Disability* is considered a negative term. But Disability does not have to be interpreted as negative. I identify as a Disabled person, which is considered "identity-first language." The word *Disabled* comes first because it connects me to an amazing community, to a history of people who have been advocating for my rights, to a collective creativity that other people don't have to have, and to laws that guarantee my inclusion. Most of the language in this devotional mirrors my preference for identity-first language for those reasons. I've also capitalized words and terms like *Disabled* and *Disability Justice* to honor that these are important parts of identity. Yet many other people also identify as "people with Disabilities" to honor their personhood first, which so many others deny. These ways of identifying show the power and pride of claiming Disability. Note, though, that each person may choose how they wish to identify. While these terms are standard, every person is entitled to their own language around their identity.

Another important perspective that I learned was the difference between the social and medical models of Disability. Historically, Disability has been understood with the medical model, which says that there is a medical "problem" that needs to be fixed. The social model, however, puts the problem on society, not on the Disabled person. For example, the medical model would assert that a wheelchair user needs medical intervention to be able to walk up a flight of stairs, while the social model acknowledges that society needs to change and put in more elevators and ramps. In another situation, the medical model would claim that an Autistic person needs therapies to stop stimming. (*Stimming* is short for "self-stimulating behaviors," which are often repetitive motions that can help someone ease anxiety or cope with emotions.) The social model would assert there is nothing wrong with an Autistic person's harmless stims, but instead people fail to accept them. Of course, while there is no perfect, all-encompassing definition of Disability, holding together these two concepts about identity and the social model of Disability can help us explain Disability in a more honorable and life-giving way.

These are some of the many lessons that I learned from my crip doulas, and I hope that they are helpful as you move forward in the new life that Disability Justice offers all of us. Lazarus has emerged, been welcomed, and been dusted off. In a similar way, may this devotional be a doula of sorts for you as we continue our Lenten journey.

CONSIDER

1. Have you heard of person-first and identity-first language? Have you heard of the social model versus medical model of Disability? What feels helpful or confusing about these two concepts?
2. How do you feel as you move into this new life that Disability Justice offers? Scared, excited, confused, welcomed? What is making you feel that way? How might those feelings influence you as you move through the rest of this devotional?

CONNECT

Write two lists of your personal identities. Which ones would you use identity-first language for? Which ones would you use person-first language for? A very brief example is: Under my identity-first list, I would have Disabled, Blind, Queer, Woman, White. Under my person-first list, I would include roommate, friend, author, artist, cook.

First Sunday of Lent

During Lent, Sunday is typically an opportunity for a break from the fast or discipline that people have been engaging in, separating that day from the rest of the Lenten season. Throughout this devotional, Sundays will be marked with time to rest, celebrate, and reflect on what the last few days have held. Each Sunday will give you space to pray several breath prayers and a longer prayer that I've written that connects several concepts of the week. The breath prayers are meant to move along with your breathing and be repeated as you breathe. As you find which ones resonate with you, continue to use them to center yourself in prayer throughout the day or week. I welcome you to come with me into God's presence in this way and rest there in these words, God's love, and your own experience of this Lenten season.

God who formed the stars,

You knew us before we were here. You felt the stars that exploded, creating the stardust that filled an empty space. You were there when we were formed and are there in all the moments of our brief, important lives. You will be there at the end, to welcome us back into the dust. Remind us that dust to dust does not mean worthless, but that we are sacred, full of glimpses of stardust and your love. Give us space this Lenten season to dust off ideas of Disability that no longer fit us and to enter into a new life filled with wisdom from the Disabled community. Give us space to dust off old assumptions of what finitude means and to recognize our finite nature as an important part of our sacredness. Remind us, too, of the sacredness of others, so we can come alongside them. In all we do, God, let us know the sacredness of humanity, the worth of dust.

Amen.

Breathe in: I am made of stardust
Breathe out: My life is sacred

Breathe in: They are made of stardust
Breathe out: Their life is sacred

Breathe in: You are the resurrection and the life
Breathe out: Resurrect my community and me

Breathe in: Jesus wept
Breathe out: And so will I

Breathe in: Finitude is sacred
Breathe out: There is worth in dust

Week 2

Created

EXCERPTS FROM EXODUS 2–4

Monday

Everyone Created Differently

READ

Exodus 2:16–22: The priest of Midian had seven daughters. They came to draw water and filled the troughs to water their father's flock. But some shepherds came and drove them away. Moses got up and came to their defense and watered their flock. When they returned to their father Reuel, he said, "How is it that you have come back so soon today?" They said, "An Egyptian helped us against the shepherds; he even drew water for us and watered the flock." He said to his daughters, "Where is he? Why did you leave the man? Invite him to share a meal." Moses agreed to stay with the man, and he gave Moses his daughter Zipporah in marriage. She bore a son, and he named him Gershom, for he said, "I have been an alien residing in a foreign land."

REFLECT

While Moses is a well-known leader in the Christian tradition, this story of Moses and the daughters of the priest of Midian doesn't often come to mind in relation to him. But it should. There are so many accounts, in Scripture and beyond, of women being taken advantage of, and it is refreshing to read about someone supporting women well. It is also interesting because at the end of this story, Moses tells us that he personally was on the margins of society. His childhood was spent as an Israelite in an Egyptian household, and he spent years in places that were not his home. His life was marked by being a stranger in a foreign land, so much so that he acknowledged this with his child's name, believed to mean "stranger" or "exile." Because he knew what it was like to be on the outside, I wonder if seeing the women being driven away made him feel connected to them. I wonder if he felt a solidarity with them. I wonder if he couldn't turn away, and wanted to stop their being treated like outsiders. Here, Moses gives another beautiful picture of what allyship means. Unlike Mary and Martha's experience, though, perhaps his allyship came from experiencing something similar to the women he encountered.

This solidarity is one of the beautiful pieces that comes from the harsh reality of being marginalized. Many marginalized groups know that solidarity is what sustains movements and helps people to find joy and love while experiencing ostracization. Liberation theologians like James Cone write about how God, too, is in solidarity with marginalized people through Jesus' life and death.[3] Cone links Jesus' death on the cross at the hands of Rome to the deaths of Black folks lynched in extrajudicial killings. He notes that true salvation comes from God's solidarity and commitment to being with us, especially those on the margins, even in the most horrifying moments. Even in this scripture story of Moses, we find God at work in solidarity with the oppressed through God's action in people.

Solidarity is an important piece of the Disabled experience. Because of this, it is a central feature on the Disability Pride flag created by activist Ann McGill and other Disabled creatives. The Disability Pride flag features a black background with five parallel, diagonal lines running from corner to corner. (The cover of this book is inspired by the flag's design.) One of the main symbols on the flag is the five colored lines running parallel to each other. Each color represents a type of Disability: red for physical Disabilities, yellow for intellectual and developmental Disabilities and Neurodivergence, white for invisible and undiagnosed Disabilities, blue for psychiatric and mental health–related Disabilities, and green for sensory Disabilities. These five colors run parallel to one another to show that though each Disabled person's experience is distinct and different, we are actively coming together in solidarity. The flag beautifully recognizes the uniqueness of each experience while still showing how Disabled people are all interconnected.

Moses's story of allyship feels particularly connected to what this flag represents because of his naming of his own marginalization. His experience as a foreign Israelite man in Egypt was likely vastly different from the lives of these seven women. They had their own hardships, their own joys, their own experiences. But Moses still entered into solidarity with them. Similarly, Disabled experiences are all vastly different depending on one's Disability. But both Moses and the women still faced discrimination, both knew the joys of someone sticking up for them, and both were tired of having to fight to feel included. Just like Disabled people, their differences, however radical, brought them together into collective solidarity. This solidarity through difference is a beautiful calling for Christians and for Disabled people. During this season of Lent, let us recognize that we are limited in our understanding of the experiences of others, but we can still come alongside them in solidarity and love.

CONSIDER

1. Who do you think has wildly different experiences from you? How can you seek to live in solidarity with them?
2. What is interesting to you about the Disability Pride flag lines, colors, and design?

3. Have you heard this story of Moses before? How does this account of his life make other, better-known stories of him read differently?

CONNECT

Spend some time considering the Disability Pride flag. Think about the distinct colors and differences between each type of Disability. Then think about how they run parallel to one another and what that sort of solidarity among differences means.

Tuesday

Created and Known

READ

Exodus 2:23–25: After a long time the king of Egypt died. The Israelites groaned under their slavery and cried out. Their cry for help rose up to God from their slavery. God heard their groaning, and God remembered his covenant with Abraham, Isaac, and Jacob. God looked upon the Israelites, and God took notice of them.

REFLECT

There are many other meaningful elements of the Disability Pride flag design. In yesterday's reflection we explored the beautiful pieces of individuality, community, and solidarity that are part of the Disabled experiences represented in our flag. Today's scripture gives us space to focus on the challenges of Disabled culture that the flag also recognizes. The parallel lines representing solidarity move diagonally down the flag from one corner to the other. This sloping movement represents the barriers of access and inclusion that Disabled people frequently face. The diagonal shows that we cannot just move forward—we are forced to move around barriers, whether physical or metaphorical. For example, when wheelchair-accessible entrances are around the back or side of a building (or not there at all), or when loud music or flashing lights prevent those with Autism or other sensory-impacting Disabilities from being in a space, Disabled people have to physically move around barriers. There are also other social barriers such as pity, harmful curiosity, shame, and fear that cause Disabled people to have to navigate around situations differently.

The black background of the flag also represents a specific experience of ableism. The black space mourns those who have been killed by caretaker violence. Everything from books like *Of Mice and Men* taught in classrooms to interviews with parents or caretakers who have committed these crimes can perpetuate the concept of "mercy killing." Mercy killings are when caretakers kill Disabled people who are dependent on them because they believe that ending their life is what is best for them, despite the caretaker's responsibility to keep the person safe. Another form of caretaker violence represented by the black space on the flag is when systems of government or community are supposed to care for Disabled people but fail to do so. One example of this is how most deaths from COVID-19 in the United States were among people with Disabilities or preexisting conditions. Governments have a responsibility to care for all members of their communities, but during the COVID-19 pandemic, many leaders enacted policies that left certain groups, Disabled folks included, vulnerable to the point of death for the sake of others not having to mask or socially distance. Regardless of the circumstance, many Disabled people have died at the hands of the people who were supposed to keep them safe.[4]

While the solidarity, individuality, and community that come with the Disabled experience are so beautiful, these two aspects of the flag are a helpful reminder that discrimination is still a significant part of our experience as well. It is important that these are represented on the Disability Pride flag, because having pride in one's identity is complex. It does not always mean being happy or excited. Instead, it means celebrating, honoring, and holding space for all parts of who we are and loving ourselves in the midst of them all. Lent is a time to recognize the pain that comes from sin in the world, and these moments of discrimination are evidence of that. By recognizing these moments, we are joining in Lenten practices of honesty and waiting—being honest about hurt in the world and waiting for something better to arrive in new life.

Throughout Scripture, God knows what those who are oppressed are experiencing, and as with the Israelites under oppression in Egypt, God comes alongside them. So many times, the experience of people who have faced ableism are lost, but the Disability Pride flag makes sure that those stories are not erased but are cried out. God's noticing the Israelites' experiences of slavery and oppression shows that their stories are not lost either. Our God is one who does not allow people's experiences to fall through the cracks. Before God goes on to act on behalf of the oppressed, we read here that God notices. God is there. God knows. And God chooses to be in solidarity with us.

CONSIDER

1. This is a heavy reflection. What are you feeling after reading it? What does your body need as you respond?
2. Why is it important that the Disability Pride flag, and the concept of pride in general, includes both the positive and negative realities of one's identity?
3. Whose cries is God listening to now? Are you listening to them too?

CONNECT

Take some time to mourn for and honor the challenges that you reflected on today. Light a candle, hold your hands open, sit in darkness, close your eyes, go on a walk, or mourn in whatever way works for you and your body. Spend time mourning those killed by caretaker violence and mourning for those who have experienced ableism. Hold space for these stories, notice these cries, and take a moment to lift up the concerns in prayer to God, recognizing that God notices, too, and we are not alone.

Wednesday

God with Creation

READ

Exodus 3:1–6: Moses was keeping the flock of his father-in-law Jethro, the priest of Midian; he led his flock beyond the wilderness and came to Mount Horeb, the mountain of God. There the angel of the LORD appeared to him in a flame of fire out of a bush; he looked, and the bush was blazing, yet it was not consumed. Then Moses said, "I must turn aside and look at this great sight and see why the bush is not burned up." When the LORD saw that he had turned aside to see, God called to him out of the bush, "Moses, Moses!" And he said, "Here I am." Then he said, "Come no closer! Remove the sandals from your feet, for the place on which you are standing is holy ground." He said further, "I am the God of your father, the God of Abraham, the God of Isaac, and the God of Jacob." And Moses hid his face, for he was afraid to look at God.

REFLECT

Some of us have read the story of God showing up in a burning bush so many times that it seems commonplace. Perhaps if we saw a burning bush today, we would even think of this story and assume God was showing up for us. But I'm sure that wasn't what Moses was thinking. When he saw the bush on fire, he was probably startled and confused. And when he tried to explain it to friends later, they were probably just as confused and maybe even skeptical of his claim that

God was really there. But still, even though it was not a way anyone had encountered God before, it was how God showed up.

When I first started studying Disability theology, I thought that the church needed to include Disabled people because it was the nice thing to do, and everyone should be welcomed. But I later realized that the church needs to include Disabled people because we are the church just as much as everyone else, and we bring something to the church that no one else does. One of my favorite examples of what Disabled people bring that others often don't is these sorts of burning bush ways of encountering God. In church spaces, we are often taught to find God in a few specific ways. This could be through prayer, scripture reading, community worship, or sometimes being in nature. Often, outside of these options, Christians don't expect to encounter God. But just like Moses may not have expected to encounter God in a burning bush, Disabled people are very aware that there is not only one way to do things.

One Disability activist, Eden from an online group called the Autisticats, explains their spirituality in this way: "At least in my own life, autistic spirituality takes the form of a heightened sensory connection to nature. Nature, in all of its patterns, fractals, and symmetries. The universe, in its conservation of mass and energy, which can only be changed, not created or destroyed. Nature in the form of the human body, which moves and spins and feels the forces that govern all existence. And so, for autistic people, stimming can be an inherently spiritual practice & experience."[5] Eden names a high sensory connection to nature, appreciation for patterns; noticing energies; and moving, spinning, and feeling the forces of the human body. All of these are deeply connected to their experience of their Autistic identity, and these are all ways that God shows up that others might not notice.

In this case and many others, Disabled people find God in ways that go beyond what is expected. Including these Disabled experiences in the church is not just a kind thing to do. It is certainly more than that. It is opening all of us up to new ways of understanding who God is and where we can find God in our lives. Whether it is in a burning bush, an Autistic stim, a Blind person's feeling of nature, or a Neurodivergent connection to others, God is showing up in beautiful and unexpected ways. These encounters can teach all of us more about who God is and the multitude of ways that we can all find to connect with God. Disabled people teach us a creativity in finding God that the church desperately needs.

As Lent continues, we wait with anticipation for Christ's resurrection and new life. Open yourself up to the next few weeks of this book, and to the mystery of the world around you, and you will start noticing glimpses of this new life in creative and unexpected places as you come alongside the Disabled community.

CONSIDER

1. What ways do you find it easiest to encounter God? What ways are hard for you? What ways would you like to explore more? Be as creative as you want with prayer, nature, service, community, Scripture, movement, and so on.
2. Are there passions or joys that are specific to you where God can or does show up in your life?

CONNECT

Today, take some time to connect with God in ways that you typically don't expect. Think about what feels good to you in your faith and broader life, and then get creative. For example, if you typically find God in nature or even just enjoy being in nature, go out and explore with your body like Eden writes about. Or if you often connect to God through prayer, go deeper and imagine you're at coffee talking with God, or take time to find and read other people's written prayer, or do something physical with your body like holding prayer beads or opening your hands to ground yourself in prayer. Consider what works best for you. It could be anything from different ways to move your body to praying imaginatively to reading Scripture creatively to connecting with others in new ways. Dive into whatever feels good to you and expect to encounter God there.

Thursday

Creating Leaders

READ

Exodus 4:1–10: Then Moses answered, "But look, they may not believe me or listen to me but say, 'The LORD did not appear to you.'" The LORD said to him, "What is that in your hand?" He said, "A staff." And he said, "Throw it on the ground." So he threw the staff on the ground, and it became a snake, and Moses drew back from it. Then the LORD said to Moses, "Reach out your hand and seize it by the tail"—so he reached out his hand and grasped it, and it became a staff in his hand—"so that they may believe that the LORD, the God of their ancestors, the God of Abraham, the God of Isaac, and the God of Jacob, has appeared to you."

Again, the LORD said to him, "Put your hand inside your cloak." He put his hand into his cloak, and when he took it out, his hand was diseased, as white as snow. Then God said, "Put your hand back into your cloak"—so he put his hand back into his cloak, and when he took it out, it was restored like the rest of his body—"If they will not believe you or heed the first sign, they may believe the second sign. If they will not believe even these two signs or listen to you, you shall take some water from the Nile and pour it on the dry ground, and the water that you shall take from the Nile will become blood on the dry ground."

But Moses said to the LORD, "O my Lord, I have never been eloquent, neither in the past nor even now that you have spoken to your servant, but I am slow of speech and slow of tongue."

REFLECT

When I was in high school, I frequently attended a summer camp with my church. It was my dream to work at that camp, but even more than that, to work at a church. I wanted to care for others and lead them to the love of God like so many leaders there had done for me. I remember one day, though, when I started to really doubt that calling. It was two years after I had started using my white cane, and there was a hill at the camp that I and a few other Disabled campers couldn't get down without assistance. I remember staying back with the others until I could grab the hand of one of my camp counselors to help me down the hill. Later, with that same counselor, I started crying and asking how I could ever be a leader in the church if I couldn't even get down a hill without someone's help.

Without realizing it, this camp, this type of church, and ultimately this culture that they created taught me that I could not lead well if I needed help. I couldn't be a good leader if there were things that I couldn't do. I was supposed to be the one giving the hand, not the one taking it. Because of the culture around me, I never thought to question why the camp was not accessible. I thought there was something wrong with *me*, not the camp. (Remember the social model of Disability.) Lent tells us that our limits are expected, human, and even sacred, but this church camp let me believe they were a burden. I hadn't considered that the church should be built on interdependence, not independence, as the body of Christ reaching out to support one another. At the time, I just wept because I thought I would not be good enough on my own because of my Disability.

Later that day, I remembered the story of Moses's call. Maybe it was God's divine intervention, or maybe it was my having paid close attention in Sunday school, but either way, I remembered Moses's words in this passage well. Moses told God that he could not be the one to speak to God's people, because he was slow of speech and slow of tongue. Most theologians agree that this is a reference to some sort of stutter or speech impediment, which means that Moses, one of the most significant leaders in the Bible, was Disabled. And even more than that, he, like me, thought that his Disability didn't make him good enough to lead God's people.

It was a life-changing moment for me to realize that God didn't choose Moses and take away his Disability. God didn't choose Moses and wish he wasn't Disabled. God didn't decide not to choose Moses because he was Disabled. God chose Moses. Period. Disability and all. God knew that Moses would be a great leader for God's people because of who he was, including his Disability. Later in the story, when Moses needs help, acknowledging that he cannot do everything on his own, God still chooses Moses. God continues throughout the Bible and history to choose Disabled leaders to lead God's people out of oppression and into God's love.

CONSIDER

1. How do you think Moses's Disability influenced his leadership? How might it have positively and negatively affected how others understood him?
2. Who are Disabled leaders that you know or have learned of? Did you learn about Disabled leaders in school or through your place of work? Or did you have to learn about them on your own? Or have you never learned of any before now?
3. Is it hard for you to recognize leadership in yourself or others when the leader is in a position of needing help?

CONNECT

There are so many amazing Disabled leaders whom we very rarely learn about in schools. Take time to do an online search and research some of them today. Here are ten names and keywords about their lives to start your search. Pick one or two (or more) and explore their work as Disabled leaders.

- Judy Heumann – "mother" of the Disability Rights movement
- Ed Roberts – "father" of the Disability Rights movement
- Brad Lomax – Disability Rights movement and the Black Panthers
- Lois Curtis – *Olmstead v. L.C.* and creativity
- Roland Johnson – Anti-institutionalization
- Alice Wong – Disability Visibility
- Leah Lakshmi Piepzna-Samarasinha – Collective care
- Stacey Park Milbern – Stacey Taught Us
- Haben Girma – Anti-ableism and law
- Stella Yong – Not Your Inspiration

Friday

Created Disabled

READ

Exodus 4:11–12: Then the LORD said to him, "Who gives speech to mortals? Who makes them mute or deaf, seeing or blind? Is it not I, the LORD? Now go, and I will be with your mouth and teach you what you are to speak."

REFLECT

This is one of the most interesting Disability-related texts in the Bible. God is speaking to the creation of Disability. It says that God not only created people with Disabilities, but also created some of those Disabilities. God is not just with Moses, but God is with Moses's mouth, the part of him that is Disabled, the part of him that God made Disabled.

In addition to the social and medical models of Disability, many Disabled activists identify a moral model of Disability that comes directly from religious spaces. For centuries, the Christian church and some other religious groups have said that Disability is a result of sin. Because many stories in Scripture feature people's assumptions that Disability comes from personal or familial sin, that belief carries over into many people's theology today. This is another area where Lent's focus on sin and bodily limitation gets linked in a harmful way. But God says numerous times that Disability is not a result of sin, especially in today's passage. God, of course, doesn't create sin, but

God does create people as Disabled. It is beautiful that God creates this diversity, and it is sad that instead of honoring it, we have chosen to assume the worst.

Lois Curtis was an incredibly creative Disabled leader. Lois was institutionalized from a young age because she was developmentally Disabled. But she fought for years with lawyer Sue Jamieson to be allowed to live in the community with a right to agency in what she did each day. The two of them won the landmark *Olmstead v. L.C.* US Supreme Court case, which led to the Olmstead Act, stating that everyone has a right to live in the community if they desire to. While there are still many people locked in institutions today, Lois's efforts require state governments to allow more people than ever before to live on their own with the supports that they need.

While Lois was living in her community, she became an artist who painted and sold pictures of people whom she loved. Her paintings were full of color and life. She named what she hoped for the people she painted who had also come out of institutions, saying, "I hope they live long lives and have their own place. I hope they make money. I hope they learn every day. I hope they meet new people, celebrate their birthdays, write letters, clean up, go to friends' houses, and drink coffee. I hope they have a good breakfast every day, call people on the phone, feel safe."[6] Lois painted the diversity and individuality that she noticed in each person, which ultimately meant that she creatively depicted an entire community.

Lois's paintings are a beautiful example of honoring the creativity in diversity and community, just as in this story of Moses and God. I wonder if, much like Lois who had hopes for a beautiful life for each person she painted, God's being with people and with their Disabilities means that God has similar hopes for us. God's creation of, and promise to be with, Disabled people means that God has hopes for us to live beautiful and full lives as Disabled people, not despite that part of us.

Instead of thinking of Disability as a negative reality linked to sin—as the church has done for many years, especially during Lent—what would it mean to think of Disability as creative, diverse, and beautiful? What would it mean to listen to this scripture and think about Disability as something created by God that God continues to be with?

CONSIDER

1. Like Lois, what hopes do you have for the Disabled community? What hopes do you think that God might have for the Disabled community? What hopes might God have for you?
2. How do you feel when reading this scripture? Is it shocking, exciting, puzzling, affirming to read that God made people Disabled?

CONNECT

Join Lois Curtis today in creatively depicting the diversity of your community. Like her, you can paint a picture of someone you love. If that option doesn't feel comfortable or appealing, you can paint or draw a picture of something that reminds you of that person or community, write a poem or song about them, or do something else creative to honor the diversity and community in your life.

Saturday

Accommodation Creation

READ

Exodus 4:13–17: But he said, "O my Lord, please send someone else." Then the anger of the Lord was kindled against Moses, and he said, "What of your brother Aaron, the Levite? I know that he can speak well; even now he is coming out to meet you, and when he sees you his heart will be glad. You shall speak to him and put the words in his mouth, and I will be with your mouth and with his mouth and will teach you what you shall do. He indeed shall speak for you to the people; he shall serve as a mouth for you, and you shall serve as God for him. Take in your hand this staff, with which you shall perform the signs."

REFLECT

When I was in college, I decided to go on a retreat with my church. I had been on many retreats in the past with different churches and had determined that they were not for me, because they had never been accessible to me. So this decision did not come lightly. People could have used flashing lights without telling me, and that would have caused pain. We could have had to read something to do an activity, and I would have been excluded. We might have watched a movie, and I would have had to go sit alone in my room. All of these things had already happened multiple times at retreats in the past year alone, so I was concerned that they would happen again. But I decided to give it one last try with a new church.

This church was different than the others had been. They knew that every part of me, eyes included, was created in the image of God, and once they learned I was coming on the retreat, they made sure that everything we did worked for me. There was not a single flashing light, fan, image, movie, or even word that I had to read. Every single game was planned in a way that not only accommodated me, but made it so that there was absolutely no difference between me and anyone else. We did several prayer exercises, all of which led us to God in new and bold ways because they were different from ones we normally would do that required vision. No one realized these were accommodations, because they included me so seamlessly, but that night I grabbed my friends, went to my room, and cried. I was amazed because I knew they noticed me. I knew they accepted me. I knew that I didn't have to fight to be included. I knew that was church and that was God. I knew that I was loved.

The past church retreats I'd experienced left me feeling like a burden, but this church honored my accommodations and, in turn, honored God. As this scripture explains, instead of agreeing with Moses that his Disability was too hard to handle, God claimed Moses's Disability as something God had created. Then God went on to accommodate Moses through Aaron. This is a beautiful story of how God is not only creative once, but over and over again to include, accommodate, and honor the particular creation of every person. God's creativity inspires me to continue to get creative about inclusion and to celebrate the creative nature of Disabled people as we continuously come up with new ways to accommodate ourselves and one another.

This story is particularly significant to the Christian and Jewish Disabled communities because it exemplifies a Disabled person who is not healed but instead is accommodated. Many times, churches assume that Disabled people all desire healing in a way that cures and erases their Disability. While some people do want that, many of us do not. The story of Moses is a reminder that God knows that Disability doesn't need to be erased. God didn't cure Moses of a speech impediment. God accommodated Moses. Sometimes, just like the accessible retreat was for me and how Moses's story turned out for him, healing doesn't mean a cure. Sometimes, healing only truly comes through accepting all of a Disabled person's identity and making room for full inclusion and accommodation.

CONSIDER

1. In what areas of your life or leadership have you needed accommodation? What feelings does it bring up for you when accommodation is done well or done poorly?
2. Does it surprise you that Moses isn't healed but is accommodated by God? Why or why not? When you think about healing, does it always mean "cure"? What would an expanded idea of healing be like that includes Disabled people and accommodation like it did for me and Moses?

CONNECT

Take a few moments to think through your plans for today or this week. What is one area where you can accommodate yourself? What is one area where you can accommodate someone else? Make it a point to do both of those throughout your day or week. As you do so, remember that accommodation is God's work too.

Second Sunday of Lent

God who creates,

God, we are spinning and twirling through fractals like Eden from the Autisticats. We are lining up in solidarity across difference like the stripes of the Disability Pride flag. We are creating our communities and listing out our hopes confidently one after another like Lois Curtis. We are learning how to be leaders while still accepting accommodations like Moses. We do all this as an attempt to create new and more welcoming realities for ourselves, our communities, and our world.

Sometimes this work feels beautiful, and sometimes it feels futile. Sometimes we brush up on our own limits, come crashing down into discrimination, or are struck by our own mourning. But you remind us that limits can be sacred, that solidarity even through discrimination can sustain us, and that we can find hope and pride only if we open ourselves to both celebration and mourning. At the borders of those limits, we can find interdependence, solidarity, accommodation, and community. In these moments, we can create community, create access, and create new ways of connecting with you.

Continue creating, God. Continue to create a world full of more solidarity and love. Continue to create accommodation, acceptance, and pride in our communities. Continue to create us, God, as we learn and grow. Help us join you in this continuous creation of ourselves, our communities, and our world.

Amen.

Breathe in: Creation is here
Breathe out: I am becoming new

Breathe in: God is at work
Breathe out: Creating in us

Breathe in: Let us create
Breathe out: Solidarity and community

Breathe in: I can find God
Breathe out: In new and creative ways

Breathe in: We are different
Breathe out: We are here together

Week 3

Blessed

GENESIS 32:24–32

Monday

Wrestling with Blessing

READ

Genesis 32:24–26: Jacob was left alone, and a man wrestled with him until daybreak. When the man saw that he did not prevail against Jacob, he struck him on the hip socket, and Jacob's hip was put out of joint as he wrestled with him. Then he said, "Let me go, for the day is breaking." But Jacob said, "I will not let you go, unless you bless me."

REFLECT

Often, when a non-Disabled person meets a Disabled person, the first thought they have is about the challenges of our Disabled identity. We get called "inspiring" for completing everyday tasks like going to the grocery store or riding the bus. We get called "God's special children" or "angels" because they don't understand the fullness of our humanity or think of us as similar to themselves. We are told that our Disabilities are a blessing, but that means a blessing for other people, to "inspire" them. These seem like genuine, nice comments, but they often make Disabled people uncomfortable. Activist Stella Young coined the term "inspiration porn" to describe this phenomenon.[7] This term explains how Disabled people's bodies and lives are used without consent to become a source of others' inspiration, sweetness, or other positive feelings. Through inspiration porn, people take our Disabilities as a blessing for themselves.

When I read about Jacob wrestling until he is blessed, I think of the many ways that I am forced to wrestle with the idea of "blessing" with my Disabled identity. For example, each time someone calls me inspiring for going to college "because I couldn't imagine going to college if I were like you," I have to wrestle the conversation in the direction I want it to go. I have to prove to them, and myself, that people "like me" belong in colleges. That also means wrestling with the school system to prove I belong there too. In those moments where people say I'm inspiring for going to school, part of me wants to say, "Instead of feeling inspired, you should feel enraged that the schools are so inaccessible" and, "You should feel empowered to advocate for Disabled people to be welcomed in that space." I want them to know that those are the actual things I have to wrestle with. I don't want people to think of my identity as a blessing because I happened to fight hard enough to make it work and that inspires them. I want my identity to be understood as a blessing enough to be included in the first place because it's an important part of who I am.

In this passage from Genesis, it also isn't surprising to me that Jacob becomes Disabled while wrestling and ends up with an injured hip. I think about the countless emails, stressful conversations, and lack of accessibility I've experienced. Wrestling with those things makes me more Disabled, too. Each of these things and many more exacerbate my chronic pain. In these moments, I realize that being Disabled is not only wrestling with people and systems, but also wrestling with our own bodies. After this wrestling match left Jacob with a limp, I wonder if he wrestled with his own identity. Suddenly he wasn't able to do everything he used to do. Suddenly his life was marked with pain. It changed who he was and what he was able to do, and he probably had to wrestle with what that meant for his life. Jacob here wrestles with finitude and limits, much like we do throughout Lent—and throughout life.

Disabled people know what a difficult switch that can be. We often end up in a place where we are wrestling with our own bodies. The real blessing of Disability comes not with inspiring others or even with feeling great about ourselves. It comes in being able to wrestle with God and with ourselves enough to find blessings in the midst of that wrestling. When we find pride, joy, and love in ourselves and our community even while accepting the pain and the challenges, then we know the true blessing of Disability.

CONSIDER

1. What parts of your identity do you feel like you have to wrestle with? What parts of your identity feel like a blessing? Are there any areas of your identity where blessing and wrestling overlap?
2. How does the concept of "inspiration porn" make you feel? What is uncomfortable about it? What parts make sense to you?
3. Does Disability feel more like wrestling or blessing to you today? What are times when it feels more like one or the other?

CONNECT

Just as Jacob wrestled with God and engaged his whole body in the act of being blessed, allow your body to connect with God today. Position your body in a posture that connects you with God—maybe out in nature, maybe comfy and safe in your bed, maybe dancing or running, maybe with your arms open or eyes closed. While situating your body toward God, think about the areas that you are wrestling with right now. Ask God to bless you there.

Tuesday

Letting Go to Be Blessed

READ

Genesis 32:26: Then he said, "Let me go, for the day is breaking." But Jacob said, "I will not let you go, unless you bless me."

REFLECT

Jacob's response to the man he is wrestling with makes sense to me. Later on, Jacob realizes that by wrestling with this man, he "came face to face with God." If I came face-to-face with God, I surely would not let go, either. I often feel like I understand almost nothing about the vastness of who God is. So, if I were to have hold of someone who was the face of God, I would definitely be holding on tight, trying to take in as much as I possibly could.

The problem, though, is that sometimes we need to let go to be blessed. Sometimes when we hold so tightly to what we understand to be the face of God, we are not getting blessed in the ways that we could if we opened ourselves up to more.

Much of my life has been wrestling with God and not wanting to let go. It started when I was in high school and my church introduced me to Emmanuel prayer. This is a way of praying where you imagine Jesus with you in one of the most positive and most negative moments of your life and think about what Jesus would do, say, and be for you in those moments. This prayer imaginatively engages with the concept of Jesus as Emmanuel, God with us. This type of prayer was life-changing for me. It was, and still is, one of the ways that I feel most connected to God and feel the most space to pray honestly. But as I was growing up, I also had other experiences with Jesus that made Emmanuel prayer complicated. Once I started using my cane, I had people continuously offering to pray for healing for me, not just at church, but at the grocery store, at school, and in restaurants. When I started using my cane, I felt like the way I was experiencing life had finally aligned with who I had always been. Regardless of whether I acknowledged it, I had always been Disabled, and using my cane was a choice I made to align with that part of myself I had ignored for so long. It honored and supported a part of me that I no longer pretended didn't exist. But this continuous pressure from adults to pray for healing kept pushing onto me their belief that they, and ultimately God, didn't want me to be that way.

As I continued to explore Emmanuel prayer, I realized that I felt extremely uncomfortable imagining myself in the presence of Jesus because of this idea of healing. Jesus was presented to me as Healer above anything else, so I was at an impossible crossroads if Jesus touched me. Either Jesus would heal me and I wouldn't be me anymore, or Jesus wouldn't heal me and he wouldn't be Jesus anymore.

This dichotomy led me to hours of discussion with my professors, my pastors, and even God. After wrestling with my faith for years, I realized that rather than hold on, I had to let go. I had to let go of the picture of Jesus that I had formed. Letting go of this view of God wasn't sinful. It wasn't heretical. It wasn't giving up on my faith. It was diving into my faith, letting go, and trusting that God would bless me if I opened myself up to encountering God face-to-face in other ways. I cried a lot, I avoided praying, and I deeply missed the false sense of comfort I had in my earlier understanding of God. But I learned that even when we let go of beliefs, understandings, practices, and images of God that limit us or no longer serve us, God will never let go of us. Letting go of those things does not mean losing God in our lives. It took years, but now I can imagine Jesus giving me a hug, sitting with me in the positive and negative, and guiding me into expansive new areas of my faith, all in ways that honor who I am and who he is. This has been an incredible blessing that I wish everyone could experience, even though it was terrifying to let go.

CONSIDER

1. What ideas and beliefs have you had to let go of during your faith journey?
2. What things have helped you feel like you were face-to-face with God?
3. Does your view of Disability seem to align with who you understand Jesus to be? Why or why not?

CONNECT

Imagine yourself with Jesus. This can be in a positive or negative moment of your life, or with you right where you are now. Think about what Jesus would do, say, or be for you in that moment. Consider what it feels like to be in Jesus' presence. Is there anything that brings up fear or discomfort? Is there anything that feels new or exciting? Is there anything you need to let go of and hand over to God?

Wednesday

The Blessing of a Name

READ

Genesis 32:27–28: [The man] said to [Jacob], "What is your name?" And he said, "Jacob." Then the man said, "You shall no longer be called Jacob, but Israel, for you have striven with God and with humans and have prevailed."

REFLECT

For many communities, including the Disability community, this passage holds a critical importance. Trans and Non-Binary folks often connect to the blessing that comes with choosing a new name that more fully honors who they are. Some Asian American, Latinx American, and other immigrant communities connect with this passage because of the change of name that can come with their journey or their parents' journey to a new country. For each of these communities, the power of a name—and specifically a change of name—is crucial. Beyond this, there are many reasons why people end up with stories about who they are related to their names. Some people do not like the name they are given at birth and change it throughout their lives. Others love their name and embrace it. Still others learn to embrace it over time or fall into patterns of nicknames that are a better fit.

Individuals in the Disabled community may not change their name, but they often find themselves changing, adding, or building upon the names they have for their Disability identity. For some people, a diagnosis is an immediate experience, whether that be at birth or after an accident. For others, it is a much longer, drawn-out process that can take months or years. A diagnosis can come as a shock that a person has to learn to live with or work to change, but it can also be a relief and even a joyful experience to find an explanation for what someone has gone through. They finally have a name for what they've been journeying through for so long, a name for the experiences they have encountered, and a name for the pieces of themselves that have not previously been named.

The man in this story who wrestled with Jacob gives him this name as a blessing in order to tell the truth about who Jacob is and proclaim the work of God in his life. The same truth-telling and prophetic witness is present in naming the Disability piece of people's identities. For many Disabled people, this is why *how* they identify their Disability is a core piece of how they understand themselves, which can change significantly as they learn more about who they are. Understanding Disability identity often takes a lot of time, effort, and change.

Lent mirrors the forty days that Jesus journeyed by himself in the wilderness, and even just in these forty days of Lent, we are growing our understanding of Disability together in new ways. Many Disabled people spend days and even years on a similar journey of finding themselves. This is why for many, self-diagnosing feels important in honoring who they are for themselves. For others, getting a professional diagnosis is important because it validates their experience and helps get them the services they need to accommodate that reality.

The terms "Disabled person" or "person with a Disability" have also become a name for some that holds the story of who they are and who their community is. Thus, euphemisms like "special needs" and "differently abled" can feel harmful because they are an attempt to rename someone's experience in ways that don't always feel truthful. Each Disabled person has a long history of how they name their own identity, so it is important to listen to yourself and those in your life about what they want to be called, not what others name them. Honoring that helps honor the fullness of their life and story, just as God does for Jacob in this renaming of who he is.

CONSIDER

1. What names for yourself or pieces of your identity have been important to you? Why? How have they shaped you? How have they changed over time?
2. Are there any pieces of your identity that have not been named or have been named in ways that you are not comfortable with? How can you invite God and yourself into the renaming process?

CONNECT

Take a moment to write an acrostic poem using your name or a piece of your identity. An acrostic poem is where you take each letter of a word or name and turn it into a word or line of poetry. Each letter can be a word or a whole phrase. For example, someone once wrote me an acrostic poem with my name, Tatum, which read "Trust, Alive, Truth, Undeniable, Miracle." Use it to name the parts of your identity that are important to you.

Thursday

Blessed by Who?

READ

Genesis 32:29–30: Then Jacob asked him, "Please tell me your name." But he said, "Why is it that you ask my name?" And there he blessed him. So Jacob called the place Peniel, saying, "For I have seen God face to face, yet my life is preserved."

REFLECT

When reading this text, I find myself asking the same question that is asked to Jacob. Why does Jacob ask for the man's name? I also wonder why he is never given an answer. This is particularly interesting because in verse 28, the man says, "You have wrestled with God," and in verse 30, Jacob says he has "seen God face to face." If Jacob knew this man was God, why did he still ask his name?

There are very few times in my life when I think I have seen God face-to-face. And honestly, depending on the day, that number changes. Some days, I think God's face shows up often, and then other days, I doubt that I have the authority to claim I have encountered God even once. I wonder if Jacob felt similarly. By claiming that this was God, he likely had a moment that he could remember and be assured in.

If the man had replied, "Oh sorry, I forgot to introduce myself, I'm God. Nice to meet you," then I bet this story would have been different. Jacob would never have named for himself that he had "seen God face to face." I think that the man's nonanswer to Jacob's question was actually part of the blessing. God allowed Jacob to be the one to name God's presence. Instead of just having confidence in what the man said, Jacob got to have confidence in himself. Every time he told the story or noticed his limp, he would know that he had "seen God face to face."

When I was younger and adults would attempt to pray my Disability away, I would stop them and say that it was actually part of who I was and that God was okay with it. But after a few times, I started assuming I should want healing, because that's what they thought God wanted. But if I had believed myself first, what might have changed? I wish I had been given the opportunity to believe my own experience of where God was. Jacob encountered God in the moment he became Disabled, and I wish I had trusted that in my own story too. To have had the confidence to name God in my experience of Disability would have truly been a blessing.

Since then, I have spent time learning to recognize God and believe it, especially through my Disability. I find the face of God in Disabled friends who just "get it." I find the face of God in Disabled leaders who have continued to fight for the love and justice we deserve. I find the face of God when I accommodate myself and others and find new ways of advocating, praying, caring for others, and living that change my perception of God, myself, and the world. I find the face of God in so many places in my communities, and I know that God is showing up in the lives of others in the same way. I pray that God gives us the confidence of Jacob to name when we have seen the face of God and not doubt our own experiences of who God is.

CONSIDER

1. Have you ever had a moment when you may have seen God face-to-face? If so, do you doubt these moments or feel confident about them? What, if anything, has made you doubt them? What, if anything, has made you more confident in them?
2. What can you do to open yourself up to finding the face of God more often? Is there anything that would help you trust yourself to identify these moments more?

CONNECT

Allow yourself to experience something absolutely lovely today. Have a dance party by yourself to your favorite song, call a friend you love, go on a walk to your favorite place, read a book that brings you peace, create a piece of art, or do something else you love. Before you start, ask God to show up in it. As you are doing it, think about how God may be working through it in your life. Consider whether you've encountered God through it before and if you are today. Trust yourself even if you find God's presence in a small way or a way that feels different to you. And if you don't feel that you've encountered God, trust yourself there as well! Don't force it, but instead find peace knowing that God sometimes works in ways that we can't identify right away.

Friday

We Know the Blesser

READ

Genesis 32:30: So Jacob called the place Peniel, saying, "For I have seen God face to face, yet my life is preserved."

REFLECT

In this story, we've read that Jacob became Disabled in his encounter with God and left walking with a limp. Most people assume that his limp went away over time, but in all likelihood he would have needed medical attention that he did not have access to in order to make it go away completely. Either way, God left Jacob more Disabled, at least for a while and maybe even throughout the rest of his life. For this reason, Jacob has an incredibly interesting experience of the connection between God and Disability. One does not exist in his story without the other. He would not be Disabled without God, and his encounter with God included the experience of Disability. Because of that, when Jacob names God's presence, it is inseparably intertwined with his Disability identity.

Yesterday we explored what this meant for Jacob's life, but this is broader than just his experience, because Jacob's identity is core to much of Christian and Jewish theology. Many times throughout Scripture and even today, God is identified as the God of Abraham, Isaac, and Jacob, or even just as the God of Jacob. This is used to testify that we are worshiping the same God as our spiritual ancestors, as a way of calling on the tradition of those who have come before us, and as a way to name the movement of God in the past and claim that God will be active today too.

Naming Jacob's Disability identity as tied up with his encounter of God is radical when thinking about this lineage. The God we pray to is the God who actively wrestled with Jacob and made him Disabled. This is also the God who, in Jesus, brought healing, which means that God engages with bodies in so many different ways, both creating Disability and healing Disability. This means that God is not just a God of the healed, but also a God of the Disabled. For many people it is easy to pray to God as healer, but it is much harder to pray to God as the God of the Disabled. But when we pray to the God of Jacob, that is what we are doing.

Many Disabled people have to wrestle with God significantly because God is presented only as healer. For those who want and receive healing, naming God as healer is wonderful, but for those who do not want healing, or those who want it but do not receive it, God as healer is not enough. Introducing the God of Jacob as the God of the Disabled makes space for a more expansive naming of the holy. It means that Disabled people can find and name God because Jacob did. It also means that God can be found in Disability, through all experiences of it, not just the assumption that healing is the only way God works. The God of Jacob is a God of the Disabled in whatever way they understand Disability to be impacting their lives. The God of Jacob is also the God of Lent, accepting finitude, limits, and bodies as they were, are, and will be. The God of Jacob is the God of our ancestors and the God of all of us.

CONSIDER

1. Is it harder for you to think of God as healer or as God of the Disabled? Why?
2. What words, images, feelings, or ideas do you use to identify God? Are there scripture passages you would want to name God in, such as God of the woman at the well or God of the cross? Or are there moments in your life that you identify God in, such as God of your child's birth, God of parents in heaven, God of miraculous healing, God of Disabled community? Consider writing a list of identities or an acrostic poem for God like you may have done in an earlier prompt.

CONNECT

God is your God just as much as God is the God of Jacob, so allow God to bless each piece of who you are. Write a blessing for yourself today. Think about how you identify God and how you identify yourself, and then name God as the God of those areas. You might choose to use the Beatitudes from the Gospels, filling in lines such as "Blessed are the peacemakers for they shall be called the children of God." Or you might draw on a prayer you've heard at your church, such as "Let God's face shine upon . . ." Or you could use something you make up that fits who you are. Pray this blessing over yourself throughout the day as you remember that God is the God of Jacob, the God of the Disabled, and the God of you.

Saturday

Disabled, Blessed, Honored

READ

Genesis 32:31–32: The sun rose upon [Jacob] as he passed Penuel, limping because of his hip. Therefore to this day the Israelites do not eat the thigh muscle that is on the hip socket, because he struck Jacob on the hip socket at the thigh muscle.

REFLECT

Jewish people do not just read about Jacob being touched by God, but honor it throughout their lives by not eating the sinew in the thigh muscles of meat. This touch was what left Jacob walking with a limp, putting him either temporarily or permanently in the Disability community. In a world that often fears or ignores Disability, this tradition powerfully honors Jacob's Disability. Many people likely don't recognize this as honoring a Disability but rather as honoring the touch of God, because of the ableist assumption that Disability is not something to honor or to connect to God's touch. Regardless, this is a moment where Disability is honored by God and by people throughout history. This is a way that the God of Jacob, the God of the Disabled, is actively remembered and honored and a way that people, intentionally or not, honor Disabled bodies.

There is a dark history in the United States and other countries of not honoring Disabled bodies. While this has happened in a multitude of ways all throughout history, one of the most evident is what are now called the "ugly laws." These laws made it illegal for people with "unsightly or disfiguring Disabilities" to be seen in public. The ugly laws were passed through the 1800s and 1900s and were in place all the way to 1974, when the last one was repealed.[8] There are many recorded instances where these laws were enforced and people were arrested and jailed simply for being Disabled in public. This horrific history is also tied up with freak shows. Freak shows, which overlapped with the ugly laws but continue in concept even today, were events where Disabled people were paraded in front of onlookers and forced to either do strange things or be observed as a strange thing in themselves. Some of these freak shows were the only opportunity for Disabled people to receive food and occasionally a few dollars and be allowed to appear in public, which made them one of the only safe choices for many people to make a living (even if this so-called living wasn't necessarily sustainable).

In a society that for years has deemed Disabled people as freaks and unsightly in this way, it is radical to think about this biblical passage. Throughout history, bodies in general have been seen as negative, and spiritual lives have been lifted up as best. It is no wonder that this is the case when for years having any sort of bodily difference led to being gawked at as a freak, being forced into isolation, or being put in jail. Bodies, then, have been understood as the enemy, when ableism should be instead. Our bodies are just as important as our spiritual well-being because our bodies are what hold us, sustain us, and ultimately *are* us. God created us as bodies, God loves us in our bodies, and God called those bodies good. Especially during Lent, it is important to name that bodies are important. Even as they move from ashes to ashes, bodies are a place where God shows up, they are people who God loves, and they are unique in their abilities and limits, all of which should be embraced during Lent and always.

The tradition of honoring Jacob's body and specifically Jacob's Disabled body is deeply countercultural. God does not erase this limp but instead honors it and tells people to honor it as well. We are reminded that God reaches out to, touches, loves, and changes bodies, even when our society chooses to shame them. Even when we are taught to fear, hate, and not trust our bodies, God shows us that we can honor every part of our bodies, even and especially those parts that are Disabled.

CONSIDER

1. Have you heard of ugly laws or freak shows? How do you feel when reading about them? How can you process those feelings?
2. Are there parts of your body that you don't honor or that you think that God wouldn't honor? What would it change if you worked toward honoring those parts and started trying to believe that God does too?

CONNECT

If you feel comfortable, look in the mirror or at a photo of yourself or think about the different parts of your body. Lay your hands on each part and name it as something to honor and as something blessed by God. You can say out loud that each part is blessed. Pay special attention to the parts that you have a hard time believing you or God should honor. If paying attention to specific parts of your body does not feel good to you, speak a blessing over yourself as a whole, or do the same activity over parts of your personality or life.

Third Sunday of Lent

God who blesses,

God who blesses Jacob, God who blesses us. Wrestle with us until we find you. Help us let go of the false ideas of you and the false ideas of ourselves and our bodies that the world and even the church has given us. There has been so much pain, God, in holding on to these easy answers. We have felt the pain that the world has caused, saying that we are not good enough as we are and that you are not who we've found you to be. Give us confidence in ourselves, our bodies, our experiences, and above all, our encounters with you. Let us join you in wrestling until we can name that we are blessed and come face-to-face with you. Help us honor the places that no one else seems to love in ourselves, in others, and in the world. You are the God of Jacob, and you are the God of us. Bless us as you did our spiritual ancestor. Bless our Disabled identity. Bless our bodies as they are. Bless the moments when we wrestle with you and where we find you. Bless our naming of ourselves and our identities. Bless us, Lord, as we wrestle this Lent with all it means to be embodied and to encounter you face-to-face.

Amen.

Breathe in: Bless us, God,
Breathe out: Face-to-face

Breathe in: Even as we wrestle
Breathe out: We find God

Breathe in: We are blessed
Breathe out: Even when others disagree

Breathe in: We are blessed
Breathe out: By God alone

Breathe in: Give us a new name, God,
Breathe out: That honors all of us

Week 4

Connected

MARK 5:25–34

Monday

Connected through Suffering

READ

Mark 5:25–26: Now there was a woman who had been suffering from a flow of blood for twelve years. She had endured much under many physicians and had spent all that she had, and she was no better but rather grew worse.

REFLECT

This week's scripture text describes a woman who not only suffered from the pain of constant bleeding and a medical system that did not have answers for her, but also faced years of isolation from her community. The woman's health condition made her ritually unclean. She was considered "untouchable" because of this ritual uncleanliness, and thus was unable to engage in much of her community's daily life.

This week, I want to focus on a significant part of Disability history as it relates to this story of the bleeding woman. The contexts are not exactly the same, of course. The woman experienced isolation because of the religious laws of her time. I want to consider how Disabled leaders in the United States pushed back against the discrimination they faced in everything from medical care to community because of their nation's laws. Before 1973, there were no civil rights protections for people with Disabilities. The passage of the Rehabilitation Act that year included a specific set of regulations, Section 504, that created and extended civil rights to people with disabilities. It was the first anti-discrimination law for Disabled people in US history.

But it took great effort to bring the legislation into reality. Political leaders stalled on signing and implementing the 504 regulations, largely because they were concerned about the projected expense of doing so. After several years of delays, Disabled activists put their bodies on the line through national protests known as the 504 Sit-in. During the sit-in, activists occupied government buildings around the country for weeks on end.

Ed Roberts, one of the sit-in leaders, had a remarkably similar story to the bleeding woman. Ed described himself as an athletic young man until age fourteen, when he became a quadriplegic. He was told by doctors, and the broader culture, that he would no longer be able to do anything that he'd dreamt of. Because of this drastic health change and the discrimination from medical professionals and community members, Ed struggled with severe depression and suicidal ideation. I wonder if the woman in today's scripture struggled in the same ways, feeling the pain of forced isolation. We know, though, that this woman gave up what the world said she needed to do and instead found hope in the presence of Jesus, something that may have felt unlikely or even impossible.

In the same way, Ed Roberts stopped listening to those who told him he couldn't participate in much of life and instead leaned into an impossible hope of something more. Ed Roberts was one of the first physically Disabled students ever to be admitted to college. He lived in the nurse's office at UC Berkeley and advocated for more Disabled students to be admitted. Eventually, he founded the Rolling Quads, a Disabled student group. He was told after graduating Berkeley that his only option was to live in a nursing home, but again he chose a hope outside of what people told him was possible. He threw himself into the independent living movement and is now considered the father of Disability Rights. He led and founded several Centers for Independent Living that continue today to assist Disabled people as they live in the community.

During the 504 Sit-in, Ed supported the protest from outside the government building in San Francisco along with hundreds of other protesters who showed up every day but couldn't sleep in the building. At the end of the sit-in, he made a powerful speech right outside the building as people flooded out. "From being people who are discriminated against daily; we've learned how to be strong," he said. "Our strength is in our unity. And our strength is in our righteousness. Because this is a cause that we've all invested our lives in."[9]

Ed Roberts, the other 504 protestors, and the bleeding woman all faced discrimination, and as Ed said, that taught them how to be strong. That strength led them to invest their lives in a hope for community and connection. Each of their hopes started a fire that burned for years, inspiring community in ways they could have never imagined. Ashes to ashes means something a little more hopeful when their fires keep on burning bright.

CONSIDER

1. What hopes do you invest your life in? How can your small actions lead to hope that ignites a lasting fire?
2. Who in your life is experiencing discrimination and isolation? You, a friend, a community? How can you help them live into a hope for community?

CONNECT

Think of someone who is dealing with pain or illness (especially one that is chronic and easily forgotten about, like that of the bleeding woman or Ed Roberts). Send this person a text or talk to them next time you see them to remind them that you're thinking of them. Do not say that you are praying for healing unless they've asked specifically for you to do so. Just convey that you are there for them. Then think about how you can include them in the future, either by inviting them to something and accommodating them in the ways they need or just in a phone call, providing a meal, or offering another mode of connection that is sustainable for their health.

Tuesday

Connected to Make Change

READ

Mark 5:27–28: She had heard about Jesus and came up behind him in the crowd and touched his cloak, for she said, "If I but touch his cloak, I will be made well."

REFLECT

The 504 Sit-in protests were the idea of Dr. Frank Bowe, a Deaf activist from Washington, DC, who was the founder and executive director of the American Coalition of Citizens with Disabilities, also known as the ACCD. When Frank Bowe learned that the 504 regulations were not being signed, he went to the ACCD board with the idea for the sit-in. After they agreed on a plan, the organization sent word to government officials that if the regulations were not signed by April 4, 1977, then the sit-in would start. They also sent word to Disabled people and Disability organizations across the country, calling on them to occupy government buildings in many different places. This included Judy Heumann, Kitty Cone, Hale Zukas, Brad Lomax, Mary Jane Owens, Ed Roberts, and others at the San Francisco office of the US Department of Health, Education, and Welfare. The HEW department had been tasked with overseeing Section 504, but the department secretary had thus far refused to sign the regulations to actually implement what the law had promised.

Dr. Frank Bowe saw what needed to happen and took matters into his own hands by writing and sending out letters about the sit-in. In our scripture today, the bleeding woman does the same. Just like Ed Roberts and Frank Bowe, the bleeding woman knew hardship and had hope enough to reach out her hand. She reached out and touched Jesus, hoping for healing. This radical hope is part of what it means to be both a Christian and an activist. Reaching out to neighbors, enemies, church and political leaders, Christ, and even ourselves in hopes of bringing healing is often what both Christians and activists are called to do.

In the 504 Sit-in, Deaf activists like Dr. Frank Bowe did this in a very specific and unique way. Deaf leaders, especially at the San Francisco building, used sign language, physically reaching out their hands, to create change. Government leaders cut off water and phone lines to most of the occupied buildings, but at the San Francisco HEW office, Deaf activists were able to communicate with the outside by using sign language through the windows. They signed things they needed like medications and food, and they also signed updates on what was happening in the building that could be shared with the media. The government could not figure out how they were communicating and thus was not able to stop their efforts, which is why the sit-in lasted for twenty-eight days, the longest sit-in in a government building in US history.

The Deaf community often calls moments like this "Deaf gain," where something is far better specifically because of a Deaf identity, sign language, or other piece of Deaf culture. This extends to the broader Disabled community as well. The 504 Sit-in is a beautiful picture of Disabled and Deaf gain, in a twenty-eight-day showing of Disabled power, community, and radical love.

These Deaf activists like Dr. Frank Bowe and many who are unnamed, just like the woman in our story, physically took matters into their own hands and were able to bring healing for the whole community through the implementation of this anti-discrimination law. The bleeding woman and these 504 activists actively claimed what they wanted and what they believed was possible by the simple and powerful act of reaching out a hand.

CONSIDER

1. What "gains" do you have based on your own individual identities and personality? What lovely and unique things are only possible because you are you?
2. How can you reach out your hand, maybe literally, to help your community or yourself today?

CONNECT

Take some time today to learn the sign language alphabet. Watch an online video created by a Deaf sign language instructor or simply search for a picture of the alphabet and learn from that. While you are learning, give thanks for this language that has led to so many Deaf gains and was the reason the 504 Sit-in was so long and successful.

Wednesday

A Healing Connection

READ

Mark 5:29: Immediately her flow of blood stopped, and she felt in her body that she was healed of her disease.

REFLECT

The bleeding woman reached out, touched God, and was healed. This verse makes it sound simple, but this woman knew that healing was complex as well. In this moment, she received a cure for her bleeding, but that wasn't all that healing meant. Touching Jesus changed her body, much like wrestling with God changed Jacob's body. More importantly, though, just as for Jacob, this change in her body changed how she thought about God, how she was included in community, and how her story and life were honored.

In a season that reminds us of our dust-to-dust reality, this story holds a glimpse of stardust in the midst. Lent is a powerful time to notice how complex healing truly is, especially when it often comes to us in beautiful little glimpses. The woman's story moves through the quick movements of her seeing Jesus, reaching out, sharing a few words, and moving on. But this moment likely stuck with her and provided more healing than a cure ever would. In Christian circles, this concept of little glimpses of healing and Christ is often called the "already but not yet" reign of God. We already have glimpses of God but are not yet living in the fullness of whatever heaven means.

That already-and-not-yet world felt true of the 504 Sit-in. Photographer HolLynn D'Lil published *Becoming Real in 24 Days*, a book containing photos she took during the sit-in of documents, conversations with government officials, key protest moments, and day-to-day sit-in life. These photos show how they were living in the already, not yet of a hope in anti-discrimination and love for Disabled people. They show images of the activists taking care of each other in the building. Protestors made sure that everyone got their medications and that everyone was turned during the night as needed so they didn't get bedsores from the mattresses or the floor. They fed, dressed, and bathed each other. They made sure that every voice was heard in every meeting, making time for sign language interpreters or those who took longer to speak. And in the midst of it all, they had wheelchair races, played games, sang protest songs, told jokes, shared stories, and had deep moments of joy. HolLynn's photos depict all of this. They show the activists living out the justice that they were fighting for in the world. They were giving a glimpse of the "already" of this love and justice while fighting for the fullness of it that had not yet been signed into law.

Like the bleeding woman touching Jesus' cloak, these moments brought healing for the Disabled community in beautiful ways, especially after the years of discrimination that had brought them there. These are little glimpses of the already in the not yet, the stardust in a dust-to-dust world. It may not be a simple cure like it was for the woman, or one quick touch bringing healing immediately. Instead, my prayer is that we find healing in the already and not yet, just like in these photographed moments of the sit-in and the memory of reaching out to Christ, because those snapshots of love and justice often bring healing far more beautiful than just a simple cure.

CONSIDER

1. Where in your life do you need a little glimpse of healing, a moment of the already while you experience the not yet? Where in your life have you found a moment like this in the past?
2. What do these reflections on the daily life at the 504 Sit-in mean for our Christian faith? How do you think healing showed up for the activists in these moments?
3. Healing, especially in stories like the bleeding woman's, is often thought to be just a cure. What other broader forms of healing can you think of that are included in this reflection or that are not mentioned here?

CONNECT

Today, spend a moment honoring HolLynn D'Lil and her photography. Take a photo of something in your life, or find a photo or image somewhere (online, in a scrapbook at home, or even in your mind) that reminds you of the already and not yet or of a glimpse of stardust in this season of dust to dust. It could be as simple as a flower or a moment with friends during the day, or you could get more creative.

Thursday

Connected to Christ's Power

READ

Mark 5:30: Immediately aware that power had gone forth from him, Jesus turned about in the crowd and said, "Who touched my cloak?"

REFLECT

Throughout the Gospels, Jesus always has power—and he uses it in unexpected ways. He eats meals with the powerless, argues with those with religious power, and is killed by powerful political leaders. So in this passage, when power flows out of him, it should make us ask what kind of power it is. To understand, we must look to the woman who received it. Jesus' power flowed out of him after he was touched by someone who was deemed untouchable. Jesus immediately recognized her need, brought healing, and reconnected her to community. Christ's power pushes against the powerful. It is a power that reaches out to touch the untouchable rather than grasp for more. Power is often used by people for personal gain, but Jesus uses it to help the powerless.

Christ's power is, of course, uniquely divine and incomparable, but glimpses of this sort of subversive power that reaches out in love can be found all over the world in different ways. This type of power was present at the 504 Sit-in, too, especially through Judy Heumann, the leader of the San Francisco occupation and the mother of the Disability Rights movement. Christ's power was rooted in his divinity and Judy Heumann's in her Disability advocacy, so their power is in some ways wildly different, but for both of them it was rooted in love, justice, and compassion.

During the 504 Sit-in, Judy allowed this deep love to flow through her in ways that Disabled people continue to admire. For example, she made sure that each person was heard. She was the organizer of the twenty-eight-day San Francisco sit-in, and many people said that she was the reason that they stayed for so long. Instead of using the power she had to dictate what they would do, each day she asked everyone individually if they would please stay one more night. She made each person feel necessary to the fight.

Judy Heumann is often remembered for sitting in front of government officials in a heated moment of advocacy during the sit-in, when she said the iconic line, "We will accept no more discussion of segregation. And I would appreciate it if you would stop shaking your head in agreement when I do not think you know what we are talking about." Judy used her role to push against power rather than to gain it for herself. She didn't try to appease the officials or cater to them; she named the important fact that they did not understand what she and the others were experiencing. She is remembered for speaking truth to power and still powerfully fighting for justice and love.

In both Judy's story and the story of the bleeding woman, power is central, but it is not the kind of power that often takes center stage. Instead, it is a radical power rooted in love. From Scripture to today, this kind of power offers us an important hope. When power flows, let it be rooted in liberation, let it be on the side of the oppressed, and let it be connected by love.

CONSIDER

1. Where, even in little ways, do you have power? How can you use it in a way that is rooted in love?

2. Even as Judy's power and Christ's power are very different, they are also linked in the pursuit of love and justice. How does it feel to think about your power as linked to all other power that is rooted in love? What other people (maybe advocates or leaders, or maybe your friends) is your power linked to?

CONNECT

Pick an area of justice that you care about and use even the little bit of power you have to push it forward in some way—write a letter to a politician, send an email to a person in power, donate five dollars (or more), tell someone something you've learned, and so on. As you do this, think of it as an addition to our collective power rooted in love that we are all working toward in little, or big, ways.

Friday

Making Connections

READ

Mark 5:31–33: And his disciples said to him, "You see the crowd pressing in on you; how can you say, 'Who touched me?'" He looked all around to see who had done it. But the woman, knowing what had happened to her, came in fear and trembling, fell down before him, and told him the whole truth.

REFLECT

What a difference it would make if this story had ended before this verse! The woman would have touched God and been cured, a lovely story of healing and Christ's power. Only, then it wouldn't have been recorded, because no one would have known except the woman herself. Then it presumably wouldn't be included in Scripture. We would also miss out on how Jesus, one verse later, speaks to the woman and calls her "Daughter." Then the woman would not have known Jesus' response to her touch.

It is so important, to the woman, to the story, and to us, that Jesus did not let the story end there. The woman reached out to him, and he paused what he was doing and reached right back out to her. It could have ended with a cure, but instead it ended with healing through full connection to Jesus and the community around her.

One of the most amazing parts of the 504 Sit-in was this connection to community. The bleeding woman was unknown, but here, people become aware of who she is, and it changes her story. During the 504 Sit-in, one of the most crucial aspects of leadership was making others aware of what the Disabled community was fighting for. It was important to let the government officials know so they would make change, and to let the media know to spread the word. And it was just as important to let other marginalized people know, people in their same crowd. This was the community surrounding them, calling them family, and reaching out to help.

The story of the 504 Sit-in cannot be told without naming Brad Lomax, the reason for many powerful connections. He helped make the cause known and drew in a crowd around the protestors. Brad was a Black Disabled man and member of both the sit-in and the Black Panther Party. It was this intersectionality, his overlapping identities, that made the sit-in so powerful. When the government started putting regulations on the HEW building in San Francisco, cutting off the water and phones and monitoring who could go in and out, Brad knew it was time to call on his community and make himself and his fellow protestors known.

The Black Panthers were integral to the sit-in effort and helped make it such a long and successful event. They publicly endorsed the sit-in. Each day, they brought hot dinners and left breakfast for the next day, as well as bringing medications and other supplies the protestors needed. They also financially supported Brad to join a group that went to Washington, DC, near the end of the sit-in to further the effort. In the words of Rev. Dr. Martin Luther King Jr., they knew that "injustice anywhere is a threat to justice everywhere,"[10] and they knew the importance of intersectional efforts. Other groups like the Butterfly Brigade, a group of gay men who helped protect people against violence, offered support as well for the same reasons. The 504 Sit-in was successful because of the marginalized communities around the protestors who formed a crowd and supported them by pausing their own work and reaching out.

What if this story had been different? What if it had ended before Brad Lomax reached out? Then they wouldn't have had food, funds, and supplies to stay in the building or go to DC. Then they wouldn't have had the support to continue. The sit-in would have collapsed. Making people aware of who they were was a necessary part of their story, just as Jesus knew it was for the bleeding woman. Love, justice, and healing often show up best in community, surrounded by a crowd.

CONSIDER

1. Who is your crowd? What parts of yourself can you make more known to them to bring love, justice, and healing?
2. Whose crowd are you in? Who can you help when they reach out? How can you be for them like Jesus reaching out and calling them family or the Black Panthers providing support?
3. How does intersectionality, or overlapping experiences in different identities, play a role in your identity? In your communities? How can you help your community become more interconnected and intersectional?

CONNECT

Today, just as Brad Lomax invited others into the fight for justice, take a moment to invite someone you know into it as well. Think of someone you know who would be helpful to or interested in the Disability Justice crowd. Reach out to them and tell them about who we are. Maybe share the story of the 504 Sit-in, invite them into an anti-ableist effort you've picked up this season, or encourage them to join in reading this devotional as well so they can learn more of who we are.

Saturday

Connected to God's Family

READ

Mark 5:34: He said to her, "Daughter, your faith has made you well; go in peace, and be healed of your disease."

REFLECT

First John 3:1 says, "See what love the Father has given us, that we should be called children of God." Our scripture today makes this love clear. It is with deep love that we are called children of God just as this woman was called daughter. We may move from ashes to ashes, but we are beloved always. People in the crowd may have been expecting the woman to be chastised for interrupting their journey or banished for touching the Son of God. At best, she may have been ignored or passed by. Yet Jesus made sure to know who she was and name her as daughter, even when the scripture writers don't name her at all. This story shows who the woman was more than anything else—a child of God—and it also reveals a lot about who Jesus is. In this moment, he is interruptible, present, and loving. He is committed to taking the time to connect with the woman rather than just moving on. This connection is core to who God is.

The 504 Sit-in was not only a beautiful point of connection for the Disabled community with each other and with the rest of the world, but for many of them, it was also a place where they had a connection with God. This Lenten season, I wanted to give multiple days to honor the 504 Sit-in specifically because the time they spent in the building also overlapped with the season of Lent, Holy Week, and Passover. Christian and Jewish protesters celebrated Passover, Lent, and Easter in the building. Lent is often a time when people give something up to open space for God in their lives, and I cannot help but think of all that the protestors gave up to be there and fight for justice. Not only did they give up their beds, homes, families, and friends during their month in the building, but they also were able to connect with God in unique ways because of what they gave up.

Dennis Billups, a Black Blind man, is often referred to as the spiritual leader of the 504 Sit-in. In a media interview, he described his own role in the movement: "I was just making sure that we had our minds together to keep going forward and don't look back. And to sing as often as we could, and to make sure that we checked on each and every other person around us, so that we could have that sense of unity. I went around the building, sometimes all night, doing cheering, doing counselling, doing listening, doing debating, that kind of stuff. I had to keep people up. I think that's what I saw as my greatest gift: that I brought in the universal aspect with the meditation and spiritualism that kept a lot of stuff together."[11] Dennis led in songs like "We Shall Not Be Moved" and "We Shall Overcome," and he offered prayer and support for everyone. Dennis Billups's leadership has been honored in the Disabled community for years, and he still often leads these songs and prayers in Disabled spaces today.

The protestors' advocacy was not complete without a connection to the spiritual, with many embracing their identities as children of God. This connection to God moved them forward in their advocacy work. So this Lenten season and always, may we know that God calls us children, just like Jesus did for this woman and just like many of the 504 protestors claimed and leaned into in their advocacy work.

CONSIDER

1. What spiritual practices make you feel like a child of God? What spiritual practices help your advocacy?
2. How has giving up time to read this devotional opened up space for you to connect with God?
3. What feelings come up for you when thinking of God calling you daughter, son, or child?

CONNECT

Because Dennis Billups led the 504 Sit-in community in songs, pick a song, poem, or book that has made you feel connected to God, your Christian community, or your worth in God. This can be a worship song or Christian book or poem, but it doesn't have to be. It can be any piece of media you love or that helps you feel connected to your spirituality. Play the song or read the poem or an excerpt from the book and consider God naming the bleeding woman Daughter, God connecting with the 504 protestors, and God's love for you.

Fourth Sunday of Lent

God who flipped tables,

We thank you for all the forms of advocacy and all the ways that people pursue justice and love. Your hands flipped over tables when people cared more about money than about their community, and your hands also reached out for the bleeding woman and many others with tenderness and care. Help us to know when we need to push and when we need to hold with care, too. Thank you for the activists who came before us who knew how to do this well. Thank you for the soft and tender moments of the 504 Sit-in: the wheelchair races, the late-night conversations waiting for everyone to be included, the counseling from Dennis, the request from Judy each evening asking if they could stay just one more day. Thank you for the strong moments full of good power, the sign language through the windows, the communities like the Black Panthers and the Butterfly Brigade sending support, and the powerful words from Judy and others to the government officials. Help us to dive into moments like these in our lives too. Help us find the already in the midst of the not yet. And most of all, call us your children and let us know that even from dust to dust, we are covered in your love.

Amen.

Breathe in: I am powerful
Breathe out: Rooted in love

Breathe in: We are powerful
Breathe out: Rooted in love

Breathe in: Let us find community
Breathe out: In the crowd

Breathe in: Jesus calls me child
Breathe out: I am held with love

Breathe in: Already we have glimpses
Breathe out: Of love that's not yet full

Week 5

Healed

JOHN 9:1–41

Monday

Healing Harmful Theologies

READ

John 9:1–3: As [Jesus] walked along, he saw a man blind from birth. His disciples asked him, "Rabbi, who sinned, this man or his parents, that he was born blind?" Jesus answered, "Neither this man nor his parents sinned; he was born blind so that God's works might be revealed in him."

REFLECT

When I was a sophomore in college, one of my professors held an "Ask Me Anything" session. Students came with everything from "Why'd you get that tattoo?" to "What is the purpose of prayer?" One student in particular thought he was really going to stump our professor by asking a hard question about whether we have bodies in heaven. My professor responded with the nuance that only she could. She named scripture passages about bodies and souls, talked through philosophers' ideas, and finally named Jesus, resurrected with a body.

When she said that, I froze. I must have made a face, because out of the thirty-some students, she turned to me and said, "Tatum, do you have a question?" I hesitated and finally asked, "If Christ resurrected with a wounded body, then what does that mean resurrection is for me, with a Disabled body?" As I've noted in earlier reflections, I knew that if Jesus healed me, I wouldn't be me, but if he didn't, he wouldn't be Jesus, so I feared her answer. But this professor said, without hesitation, "What would it mean for your body to be surrounded in unconditional love?"

I remember holding back tears. In that one question, she let me be me and God be God in the exact way that I needed. She undid the harmful theology of Christ as healer and eraser of Disabled bodies and gave me a framework for a God of love who loved my body, whatever that meant for me.

Our scripture passage today has since been one of my favorites because it reminds me so much of this moment. "Who sinned, this man or his parents, that he was born blind?" the disciples asked. But Jesus said no to their bad theology. Jesus said, "Neither this man nor his parents sinned; he was born blind so that God's works might be revealed in him." This comment took their bad theology, which linked Disability to sin, and flipped it, like my professor did for me, saying that his Disability was instead linked to the work of God.

Many people interpret this passage to mean that the healing of the Blind man was the only way God's work was revealed. But the text does not say, "This man will be healed so that God's work might be revealed." Instead, it says that he was "born blind so that God's work might be revealed." God's work is not just curing the man's blindness. It starts the moment he was born and is revealed through his blindness all his life. In this story, the Blind man reveals God's work of teaching, preaching, courage, faith, and more. If we consider God's work just the healing, we miss God's many other revelations to us in this text.

When my professor asked what it would mean for me to feel unconditionally loved, I realized that God's work shows up in love for all of who I am. As a Disabled person, I realized that this type of love is not only present for me, but through me, as one of the ways that God is revealed. Because I knew the importance of accepting all of who I was, I was able to live out that love for others. This work of God would not be revealed if I still considered healing to be the only way God is working. This story of the Blind man and my story, contemplating my own Blindness, reveal God's work in so many ways, much deeper than what we initially assume.

CONSIDER

1. Where is the work of God revealed through you? Where has the work of God been revealed through the Disabled community so far this Lent?
2. Have you ever healed from a bad theology? What feelings did that bring up for you? What changed about how God is revealed to you now?

CONNECT

Today, take a moment to create your own breath prayer and pray it throughout the day. You can fill in the blank with things about who you are. Inhale "I am ______ so that," and exhale "the work of God is revealed in me." You can fill in the blank with parts of your identity, like Disabled, Latina, Sister, or Teacher; with personality traits, like loving, brave, or silly; with things you like to do, like cooking or art; or with anything else that feels true to you.

Tuesday

Healing, Just Healing

READ

John 9:5–7: "As long as I am in the world, I am the light of the world." When [Jesus] had said this, he spat on the ground and made mud with the saliva and spread the mud on the man's eyes, saying to him, "Go, wash in the pool of Siloam" (which means Sent). Then he went and washed and came back able to see.

REFLECT

Stories of healing like this one are one of the biggest topics of Disability theology and justice in the church. These stories have caused both hope and pain for the Disabled community because they are so deeply tied to our bodily experience. To be Disabled often means automatically being linked to the idea of cure or healing. This is because so much of how we understand Disability comes from the medical model and emphasizes a need for bodies to fit social structures rather than for society to make space for them. Even those who have never wanted a cure for themselves are pressured by those around them to want healing. They are often told to desire a non-disabled "ideal" by family, friends, and even strangers. Bible stories about healing make that link even clearer. When a healing story is read in church, or a healing service is performed, the congregation often turns to Disabled people in the room, either actively or at least in their minds.

But what if the "healing stories" weren't such a separate category? What if they weren't separated out from the rest of God's work? Throughout Scripture, God is healing, and throughout Scripture, God engages with bodies in so many other ways. Instead of naming just the "healing stories" as a category of how God works in the world, I've embraced the idea of "changing stories," where God doesn't just heal bodies, but changes bodies. This concept broadens God's work and shows that God's love takes many forms, rather than just a one-size-fits-all cure.

This story of the Blind man has a very clear healing component. Jesus puts the mud on the man's eyes, the man goes to the pool to wash, and he comes back able to see. There are so many stories like this of people who are Blind, Deaf, Non-speaking, or physically or mentally Disabled all throughout the Bible and throughout Christian tradition. These stories are important to hold, honor, and hope for if that's what people want for themselves. But there is also so much more. There are stories like Jacob's, where God connects with him and he becomes more Disabled. The apostle Paul is made blind by God and then has a "thorn" that many theologians believe was a lingering visual impairment or other Disability. God also makes Zechariah temporarily Non-speaking when he doesn't believe the coming birth of his son John the Baptist and introduces Disability to others as well. Then there are the stories like of Moses or Zacchaeus, where God provides accommodations to support their bodies as they are. These stories of disabling and accommodating are just as important as curing. We know that God's work is displayed in the healing of the Blind man and others, and this truth is wonderful for many people. But it is not complete without the reality that God's work is also displayed through a variety of ways that God changes and loves all bodies.

This Lenten season gives us time to reflect on bodies. It gives space to consider the finite, limited, and time-stamped reality of our bodies. It allows us to give thanks for that very thing, that our bodies are changing, are shifting, and are moving from ashes to ashes, but are also holding a world of possibilities in between. Let God meet us there, whether that be healing, disabling, accommodating, or changing us in some other way, knowing that in all of these, we are loved.

CONSIDER

1. Have you ever had a healing encounter with God? Have you ever had an accommodating, disabling, or changing encounter with God?
2. When you've heard stories of healing, have they felt like they were in a separate category from other parts of Scripture? If so, what would be different if they had been included with the rest? If not, what helped make that reading so inclusive of all Scripture? How can you encourage that in other church spaces?

CONNECT

Say a prayer today for someone in your life who needs (and wants) healing, while honoring that a cure is sometimes the way that God works. In the same prayer, pray for another person (or group of people) with an openness to God working in their life through their own Disability, in accommodation, or changing their body in some way. Welcome space for God's work to be displayed in a multitude of ways.

Wednesday

The Opposite of Healing

READ

John 9:8–17: The neighbors and those who had seen him before as a beggar began to ask, "Is this not the man who used to sit and beg?" Some were saying, "It is he." Others were saying, "No, but it is someone like him." He kept saying, "I am he." But they kept asking him, "Then how were your eyes opened?" He answered, "The man called Jesus made mud, spread it on my eyes, and said to me, 'Go to Siloam and wash.' Then I went and washed and received my sight." They said to him, "Where is he?" He said, "I do not know."

They brought to the Pharisees the man who had formerly been blind. Now it was a Sabbath day when Jesus made the mud and opened his eyes. Then the Pharisees also began to ask him how he had received his sight. He said to them, "He put mud on my eyes. Then I washed, and now I see." Some of the Pharisees said, "This man is not from God, for he does not observe the Sabbath." Others said, "How can a man who is a sinner perform such signs?" And they were divided. So they said again to the blind man, "What do you say about him? It was your eyes he opened." He said, "He is a prophet."

REFLECT

Sadly, this story of disbelief and invalidation didn't stop back in biblical times. Many Disabled people who read this passage are struck by how true it feels to their own experience of trying to prove their Disabled identity and access needs to everyone from schools and medical professionals to families, friends, and church communities. This Blind man had people doubt his experiences, who he was, and if he was ever really Blind. These doubts remain today in everything from teachers and employers questioning, "Do you really need that accommodation?" to doctors and families asking, "Are you making it up?" and strangers probing, "Can't yoga just fix it?"

One of the times that this doubt reared its ugly head was in response to the 1990 Americans with Disabilities Act, also known as the ADA. This law was established after Section 504 of the Rehabilitation Act, which we discussed last week. While 504 was a few sentences instituting anti-discrimination, the ADA provided detailed rules and regulations around accommodation, accessibility, and other legal supports. As Disabled leaders like Justin Dart started advocating for this law, they received tremendous pushback, some in the form of the same disbelief the man in this week's scripture received. "Why does our building need to be accessible if Disabled people don't come?" "Won't it ruin our historic look?" "Do people actually need these things?" "Can't they just make it work themselves?"

In Scripture, the Blind man is questioned repeatedly and tells his story just as often. One of the most powerful moments is when he simply states, "I am he," claiming in that sentence all that he has continued to say is true of him. When the Americans with Disabilities Act was passed in 1990, Disabled activists also took a moment to say, "This is me, I'm Disabled, and I'm the one who needs these accommodations." That moment went down in history as the Capitol Crawl.

Over one thousand Disabled people rallied together at the US Capitol building in DC and put their bodies on the line to show how inaccessible the country really was. The Capitol building only had large staircases at its entrance, making it so that Disabled people both literally and metaphorically could not access their country and its government. So these one thousand Disabled activists demonstrated this reality by getting out of their wheelchairs and setting aside their other mobility aides and crawling up the steps. The activists were there to show exactly how necessary the ADA was, especially to those who doubted its importance. The protestors shared their stories and experiences with a physical display of inaccessibility much like the Blind man verbally shared his truth with those in doubt.

In this place of doubt, disbelief, and invalidation, especially when it comes to people's identities and lived experience, it's helpful to remember those who have come before, validating it along the way. Whether it's the Blind man's story or those at the Capitol Crawl, people have spent years saying, "My experience is valid." Their acts of courage give us space to say, "Mine is too, and so is my neighbor's."

CONSIDER

1. When and how have you encountered people doubting your lived experience? What feelings did that bring up for you then and now? How does hearing the stories of the Blind man and the Capitol Crawl affect those feelings?
2. Had you learned about the Capitol Crawl before? What struck you as interesting about it then or today?

CONNECT

Remember a moment when you felt like people doubted or questioned your lived experience. Find a photo of yourself from around that time or bring to mind your own picture or feeling of yourself in that moment. Imagine yourself or God saying, "I believe you," validating your experience, and listening to your story. If you're comfortable, imagine the Blind man as well as Justin Dart and other protestors at the Capitol Crawl saying, "I believe you" as well, widening your sense of community with those who've gone before.

Thursday

Healing Relationships with Parents

READ

John 9:18–23: The Jews did not believe that [the man] had been blind and had received his sight until they called the parents of the man who had received his sight and asked them, "Is this your son, who you say was born blind? How then does he now see?" His parents answered, "We know that this is our son and that he was born blind, but we do not know how it is that now he sees, nor do we know who opened his eyes. Ask him; he is of age. He will speak for himself." His parents said this because they were afraid of the Jews, for the Jews had already agreed that anyone who confessed Jesus to be the Messiah would be put out of the synagogue. Therefore his parents said, "He is of age; ask him."

REFLECT

Parental relationships are often complex and multifaceted, and this can especially be the case for Disabled people. As with any relationship, there is a wide spectrum of experiences. While some people learn Disability pride and advocacy from their parents or caregivers, others may experience doubt and questioning from their family, or even violence and fear. It is crucial that all of these are acknowledged as potential parts of the Disabled experience.

Today's text is another scripture passage that Disabled people can identify with. Relationships with parents and caregivers are a significant part of the Disabled experience. Many parents create a sense of pride in who their child is as a Disabled person. For this reason, it seems important to consider again the significance of the Disability Pride flag. As noted in previous reflections, the flag's colored lines represent different identities, their parallel nature represents solidarity, and their diagonal orientation moving around barriers and ableism. Many caregivers understand the flag's significance to the community and work to instill pride in their children in beautiful ways.

However, the flag's black background signifies the mourning in our community for those who have been harmed or killed by caretakers and parents in mercy killings. Many parents and caregivers have taken their child's life because of their ableist belief that their life is too hard to manage or not worth living. Both these positive and negative realities show the strong impact of parental relationships on the Disabled community. So while reflecting on the Blind man's own parental relationship, let us mourn the ways that Disabled people have been harmed by those closest to them and celebrate the hope we have in communities who instill Disability pride.

In this story of the Blind man, the people do not believe him and seek to talk to his parents. Often, people will believe non-Disabled people about a Disabled person's experience before believing the person themselves, even for things as simple as a waitstaff asking, "What would she like to eat?" As seen in this story from Scripture, the non-Disabled people did not reply in the way that the Disabled person himself would have—namely, the Blind man insists on telling the truth of who he is while his parents bounce around the truth. This shows the incredible importance of talking directly to and believing Disabled people rather than a parent or friend. For non-Disabled allies, it is important to recognize this and allow Disabled people to speak for themselves. Simultaneously, it is helpful for non-Disabled allies to advocate against ableism and for accessibility because they have an easier time being believed and less of a personal burden tied to that advocacy work.

Finally, it is interesting that in this scripture passage, the parents say, "Ask him; he is of age." Of course, believing their son is what would have been best in the first place. Many interpreters of Scripture name that this is what the parents are trying to encourage. Today, this type of phrase is often a helpful tool to use to support a Disabled friend or family member. However, this passage notes that the parents say this out of fear. Advocating for their child could lead them to the same excommunication he faces, so their fear is valid. However, that fear should not tear them away from allyship. These parents lack the Blind man's courage to name the truth of his Disabled experience. I pray that we as Disabled and non-Disabled people alike have the courage to overcome our fear, tell our stories, encourage Disabled experiences to be believed, and combat ableism.

CONSIDER

1. In the scripture text, which part of the parents' involvement is most striking to you? Why?
2. If you are a Disabled person, do you feel comfortable trusting a few specific people to advocate on your behalf? How can you invite them into that? In what areas do you feel the need to advocate for yourself, and in what areas can you trust others to advocate for you to alleviate some of the burden?
3. If you are a non-Disabled person, how can you overcome your fear and advocate against ablesim? How can you encourage people to listen to and believe Disabled experience?

CONNECT

Write out or speak aloud a note to your parent, a caregiver, or a mentor, sharing with them what you wish they could understand about you, or something you are grateful that they understand already. Afterward, you could share it with them or choose just to keep it for yourself as a reminder that what you want to share is valid even if they can't or won't listen.

Friday

Other Healing Works of God

READ

John 9:24–34 (NIV): A second time they summoned the man who had been blind. "Give glory to God by telling the truth," they said. "We know this man is a sinner."

He replied, "Whether he is a sinner or not, I don't know. One thing I do know. I was blind but now I see!"

Then they asked him, "What did he do to you? How did he open your eyes?"

He answered, "I have told you already and you did not listen. Why do you want to hear it again? Do you want to become his disciples too?"

Then they hurled insults at him and said, "You are this fellow's disciple! We are disciples of Moses! We know that God spoke to Moses, but as for this fellow, we don't even know where he comes from."

The man answered, "Now that is remarkable! You don't know where he comes from, yet he opened my eyes. We know that God does not listen to sinners. He listens to the godly person who does his will. Nobody has ever heard of opening the eyes of a man born blind. If this man were not from God, he could do nothing."

To this they replied, "You were steeped in sin at birth; how dare you lecture us!" And they threw him out.

REFLECT

During Lent, we are given space to question our theology and think about God in new ways. So often, churches have presented God in a beautiful little box, filling us with joy and hope on the happy days and sweet platitudes for those not-so-good days. But Lent is a time when we get to come face-to-face with the bad days, the Jesus-in-the-tomb days, the days where joy and hope feel light years away.

So, during Lent and all year, we can embrace this and find God in other places than where we expect. This week's John 9 passage allows for that better than most, giving us forty-one verses of a story where God is showing up all around the finitude and messiness. God's work is accounted for through Jesus when he says that this man "was born blind so that God's works might be revealed in him" (v. 3). This work is being revealed left and right in this story. But just like God's work in the messiness of Lent, this work is also different from what the religious leaders and community expect.

In the story so far, the Blind man has been healed, which shows God's work clearly, but in a way that feels expected to many of us today. In addition, two days ago, we read about the man telling the truth and speaking truth to power. As he tells his story, he normalizes Disabled experience, honors the work of Christ, and speaks a truth that is life-changing for him—and for the others if they would allow it to be. In yesterday's reading, we discussed how God's work of courage is also present in the man's life. His parents do not hold the courage that God has gifted the Blind man, and with that courage he is able to do these great works.

In today's passage, though, God's work is revealed through him even more clearly. First, the Blind man, after some more truth-telling about his own experience with Jesus, asks the others if they want to become disciples. Even in the intensity of this moment, he is doing the work of disciple-making and encouraging those around him to follow Christ.

The man also goes on to say, "I have told you already and you did not listen. Why do you want to hear it again?" This reminds me of Judy Heumann's iconic line at the 504 Sit-in: "I would appreciate it if you would stop shaking your head in agreement when I do not think you know what we are talking about." These are both powerful moments of boundary-setting, especially in the face of discrimination. The activists' work of honoring themselves, and the Blind man choosing to stop repeating his story when the people aren't listening, are also powerful works of God. Jesus tells us to love others as we love ourselves. Loving ourselves can truly be an imprint of God's work and love in the world, especially when the love from those around us is lacking.

In the latter part of this passage, the Blind man teaches, or more accurately preaches, the glory, power, and godliness of who Jesus is. This gift, especially in the face of those who could and did excommunicate him, is a beautiful act of God's work through him. Over and over again, this man reveals the work of God, not just through healing, but through forty-one verses of truth, power, courage, teaching, preaching, disciple-making, and more.

CONSIDER

1. Where is God's work being revealed in your life? In the lives of those around you? Especially in areas or ways you are not expecting?
2. What work of God through the Blind man do you most relate to in your experience of God? Which way is new to you or one that you don't often think of God working in?

CONNECT

All of these works listed provide healing in some way—healing the Blind man's self-respect and love, healing the community around him, healing through following Christ. Do something today that brings healing to one area of your life: take a bath, take a walk, have a conversation with a friend, forgive yourself or someone else, celebrate something, write a note to your past self, and so on. Choose anything that feels healing for you, and know that it is a work of God

Saturday

Encountering the Healer

READ

John 9:35–41: Jesus heard that they had driven [the man] out, and when he found him he said, "Do you believe in the Son of Man?" He answered, "And who is he, sir? Tell me, so that I may believe in him." Jesus said to him, "You have seen him, and the one speaking with you is he." He said, "Lord, I believe." And he worshiped him. Jesus said, "I came into this world for judgment, so that those who do not see may see and those who do see may become blind." Some of the Pharisees who were with him heard this and said to him, "Surely we are not blind, are we?" Jesus said to them, "If you were blind, you would not have sin. But now that you say, 'We see,' your sin remains."

REFLECT

This passage is both beautiful and troubling for Disabled people. There is beauty in the connection that Jesus makes with the Blind man, choosing to be on his side of the exile. Yet there is pain in the moment that Jesus uses Blindness as a negative metaphor.

As a Blind person, it is startling, and even hurtful, to hear Blindness used by Jesus in this way. Jesus says that those who are Blind can metaphorically "see" and those who are sighted are metaphorically "Blind." Jesus chooses to use a metaphorical "Blind" to mean ignorant, and "sighted" to mean blessed and aware. Ableist language like this is so common in Scripture and in our lives. Often, when a word like *Blind* is used to mean ignorant, or *insane* to mean wild, these ideas get tied together unconsciously. These word choices become internalized and lead to harmful actions, such as when strangers first meet Blind people and talk in a baby voice, assuming ignorance. Or when people learn someone has a mental illness (long ago diagnosed as insanity), they assume the person is wild and uncontrolled. After so often associating a Disability identity with something negative, when people encounter a Disabled person, the association comes out. Jesus' metaphor perpetuates this even as he is attempting to flip it around.

Jesus is still attempting to shift it in some meaningful ways, though. When Jesus talks about those who are physically Blind and sighted, it is those who are Blind who are blessed or "sighted," and those who are sighted who are unaware or "Blind." This powerfully upends the idea that Blindness is a sin or problem and names it as a positive. Though the metaphor may be hard to encounter today, Jesus' naming specifically that those who are Blind are able to understand (especially God) best is a huge move to make on the side of the Disabled community.

Throughout these weeks of Lent, we have touched on biblical and contemporary figures who have been fierce allies on behalf of the Disabled community. In this moment both in and before the metaphor, we get to receive Jesus on our side as an ally as well. Jesus notices the dividing line that the community made, placing the Blind man on the other side with him both physically and with his words. Instead of sticking with the religious leaders, Jesus chooses to cross the line and be on the side of the oppressed.

Being a Christian often means following Christ to that side of the dividing line. It is on that side of the line that Jesus reveals who he is.

It is on that side of the line that the Blind man understands far more than the others. When we find Jesus on that side, God is revealed more fully, and Jesus' identity is understood.

Often, when there are sides like this, the side of the oppressed is the most honest. It can hold the fullness of who people are and who God is. The side of the oppressed is where we can come together and find faith, whether we are the ones who were forced across or those who chose to move to that side. A professor once told me that following Jesus means always being all for the most marginalized person in the room. Though his language or actions may be different from what we expect, Jesus is no doubt modeling that here. It is our job to follow him to that side and answer his call.

CONSIDER

1. Does this passage or other passages of Scripture frustrate you? Does it feel comfortable for you to feel confused or hurt by God's action in the Bible? Or does that feel uncomfortable? What might being honest about these frustrations do for your faith?
2. Where can you choose to be on the side of the oppressed? How can you make that choice practically in your life? Who has chosen to be on your side when you have experienced harm or discrimination?

CONNECT

Think of one negative way (or ways) that you use an ableist word or phrase in your vocabulary and switch it out for something that is not someone's lived experience. (Common examples are switching *crazy* for *wild*, *Blind* for *ignorant*, *freak out* for *be chaotic*, or *Bipolar* for *emotional*). Of course, you can use *Blind* or *Bipolar* when referring to an actual Disability, but not as a negative metaphor for something else. Then, think of a positive (but not patronizing) metaphor for Disability (examples can be a white cane reaching out to connect to the world, wheelchairs being a form of freedom, or noise-canceling headphones providing safety or peace). Try to find a place to use this metaphor in your day.

Fifth Sunday of Lent

God who works in more ways than we could imagine,

Work in us, through us, and around us. Show up here in the places we are trying to find you and the places where we would never expect you to be. Work through us in all of the beautiful parts of who you made us to be, and work through us in the areas of ourselves that we didn't know we could trust you with. Work through us like you did the Blind man. Help us to be truthful, like the Blind man telling his story and the Capitol Crawl protestors naming their needs. Help us have courage to tell our story, to name where you show up, and to advocate for others. Help us preach and teach, or listen to preaching and teaching, in ways that are always on the side of the oppressed. Help us be always on the side of the oppressed. Help us notice you in the healing, and also the disabling and accommodating. Help us recognize you in our changing bodies even when we have a hard time with those changes. In this season of Lent, open us up to new ways of finding you working in the world and in us. Thank you for showing us the holiness of ourselves and our world even in the places we don't think it will show up. Thank you for working in ways we could never expect and allowing us to find you there. Meet us in those unexpected places this Lent and always. We are waiting. We are excited to find you there.

Amen.

Breathe in: I am ______ so that
Breathe out: The work of God is revealed in me

Breathe in: You are showing up
Breathe out: In the unexpected places

Breathe in: Help me find you
Breathe out: In the unexpected places

Breathe in: God is working
Breathe out: On my side

Breathe in: I will follow Christ
Breathe out: To the side of the oppressed

Week 6

Anointed

MATTHEW 26:6–13

Monday

Anointing Happens at the Margins

READ

Matthew 26:6: Now while Jesus was at Bethany in the house of Simon the leper . . .

REFLECT

In Scripture and history, lepers are greatly marginalized due to their physical condition. Not only were they deemed unclean, but so was everything they touched and sometimes even every place they went. But Jesus went there. Jesus was at the home of a Leper. Jesus was at the home of a Disabled man. And Jesus continues to be in the homes of Disabled people.

Homes like these are some of my favorite pieces of Disability history and culture. I spent three wonderful years living in the Duke Divinity School Friendship House, one of a few homes connected to several seminaries devoted to allowing people with intellectual and developmental Disabilities to live in the community rather than an institution. In a state where five to six thousand people are dealing with institutionalization or the threat of it, Friendship House and other houses like it know the importance of even the little moments of community living. I will forever remember the weekly dinner and prayer times, movie nights and dance parties, long talks on my bedroom floor, walks to coffee shops, birthday celebrations, and hours spent on the couch watching *Friends* or *Jeopardy* together. These are the moments that all people deserve, and in Disabled-centered houses, these moments feel just a little more sacred because we know their worth.

Friendship House is not the only space where the beauty of Disabled housing shows up. Activist Stacey Park Milbern was an amazing leader in the Disability Justice movement. In the years before her death in 2020, she formed a group called the Disability Justice Culture Club right in her home. The DJCC is a hub for community and organizing work. The club describes its many uses: "storage and distribution for DJCC's various mutual aid projects; a venue for fundraising events, holiday celebrations, and parties for and by the local disabled community; emergency housing for sick and disabled folks during wildfire evacuations, power outages, and other climate crises; sign-making parties and tactical meetings for direct action; and as a classroom, theatre, and kitchen [for movement work]."[12]

One of Stacey's good friends was Leah Lakshmi Piepzna-Samarasinha. Piepzna-Samarasinha describes another home similar to Stacey's. Her friend M lived in a house where "poor, multiracial, queer, Disabled people would hang out, support each other, plot and laugh. For years [M] held Friday night dinners where anyone could come over and eat some chicken. He would always talk to me about how important it was to him to center the least popular crips. The ones who were cranky, angry, difficult, crazy in ways that even other crazy people shied away from. He wanted the people who had the least community because of all the ways that ableism kills through isolation, to feel home."[13]

Disability housing appreciates the value of community living in ways that others do not have to. People in these houses know how easy it can be to lose these community moments and be forced into institutions, so these moments are cherished. The little moments are full of the joy of connection that was fought for. The care and love that comes from living in the community is celebrated boldly and unapologetically in ways that other homes miss. As we continue to read this story of Jesus at the home of a Leper, consider the importance of this location. In this season of Lent, honor the finitude of our time with each other. Celebrate and cultivate the little moments of community like Disabled people do so well.

CONSIDER

1. Do you have a Disabled home in your area like the ones described in this reflection? If you're unsure, try searching online for L'Arche, Friendship Houses, or Disability housing in your area. How can you connect with or support them?
2. How do you think about your housing situation? Do you relate to the stories of Friendship House, the DJCC, or M's dinners? Can you use the space you have to create some of these community-honoring moments?

CONNECT

At some point today or this week, cook a meal (or provide a snack, game to play, letter, or some other act of community and care) for the people in your house or other people around you. This could be your family, friends, roommates, coworkers, neighbors, church, fellow students, or any other group of people you find yourself connecting with regularly.

Tuesday

Who We Are Anointing

READ

Matthew 26:7: A woman came to [Jesus] with an alabaster jar of very costly ointment, and she poured it on his head as he sat at the table.

REFLECT

A few verses later in this Matthew 26 text, Jesus says this anointing has prepared him for burial, similar to how bodies that have just died are prepared. But here, a woman chooses to anoint a living person in the middle of dinner. This startling situation leaves readers with a lot to consider. One of the biggest questions people ask is, Why? Why did she anoint him here? Why didn't she wait till he died? Why did she use so much oil when it was so expensive? Why did Jesus need anointing?

While many have speculated on these questions for centuries, most theologians can agree that this woman was committed to honoring Jesus. She gave up this costly ointment and poured it on his head as an act of respect, care, and reverence. These acts are often done when someone has already died, but this woman knew even before death how important it was to care for and honor the body of Christ.

During Lent, this act of anointing helps make sense of a complicated season, just as it likely helps the woman and the others there make sense of the complicated reality of Jesus' approaching death. Our bodies are finite and are moving toward death. The bodies of those who came before us have already been buried. But in between, there are moments of anointing.

During this Lenten season, I pray that we can also know the importance of honoring bodies before and after death. Taking the time to care for the bodies around us is part of embracing and cherishing our finitude and community. Just as the woman cared so well for Christ's body, we are called to care for and honor our bodies and the bodies of our friends and neighbors—even when it's impractical, unexpected, and doesn't quite make sense. I hope that this book helps people honor their bodies, the bodies around them, and the bodies that came before, especially in a culture that asks, "Why?"

People ask, Why can't you work harder? Why do you need that accommodation? Why do you need self-care? Why are you making a big deal of your needs or accomplishments? Why are you spending so much time helping them? I hope that we have the capacity to respond much like this woman by choosing to care for ourselves and others even when it is unexpected. I hope we know the worth of our bodies and the bodies around us. I hope we honor them with love, accommodation, support, and celebration, even when the world wants us to ignore them and work harder and faster.

In the same way, when an important person in our lives dies or when we honor someone from history, people may ask, Why are you grieving for so long? Why are they still relevant when the world is moving on? Why can't we just focus on people doing the work now? But these bodies deserve anointing too. They deserve to be celebrated and remembered. I hope that this Lent, we remember those who went before in the Disability Rights and Justice movements and honor their legacy. I hope we honor the lives of those we were close to and those we never knew but who influenced our own. I hope we can say their names, tell their stories, build on their work, and celebrate their legacies. Especially during this season when we focus on bodies and death, I hope that like this woman, we ask why anointing is only for the moment between death and burial. I hope we extend that honor to bodies now and bodies that came before.

CONSIDER

1. Whom in your life does it feel important to honor, anoint, respect, or care for?
2. How can you anoint and honor yourself? Your friends and neighbors? Your loved ones who have passed? Those that have formed the history of your community? Now and in an ongoing way?
3. Do you often choose to honor those who are living or those who have passed? Do you move on quickly from either act of remembrance? Why?

CONNECT

Get some oil (olive oil or vegetable oil is fine) or water and make the sign of the cross on your forehead. Let it be a moment where you commit to honoring your body, the bodies of others, and the bodies who came before you. Think of someone in your life now and someone who has passed away whom you'd also like to honor. Imagine yourself anointing them as well, or dab an image or item of theirs with the water or oil you anointed yourself with. Commit to caring for yourself, for the living person, and for the other's memory.

Wednesday

Not Quite Anointed Behavior

READ

Matthew 26:8–10: But when the disciples saw it, they were angry and said, "Why this waste? For this ointment could have been sold for a large sum and the money given to the poor." But Jesus, aware of this, said to them, "Why do you trouble the woman? She has performed a good service for me."

REFLECT

This moment of the story takes the spotlight off the woman and Jesus. It moves over to the disciples for a moment of confusion and even conflict. They look at the woman's radical act and say, "This is a waste." They are watching the way that she is honoring Jesus, and they say, "You should not have done this." Knowing that Jesus goes on to tell them that the woman is correct in her action makes this moment even more interesting.

Clearly, the disciples were not contradicting her to be rude or to act like they knew better. They wanted the money to go to the poor. Which is a lovely thing, especially because they had spent years with Jesus, sharing life with the poor and marginalized, and so they likely knew the great need and were trying to practically help the people that they cared for. They were making a choice that felt the most loving to them, using the resources they had to support others. Only,

Jesus still said the woman was right. He still knew that what the woman did was important. Even though the disciples were trying to help, he said that they were wrong.

If I'm being honest, this feels relatable all too often—when I try to do something helpful only to realize that it's not quite right. In the context of Disability, I remember times when I've asked questions, changed my tone of voice or been patronizing in other ways, and made assumptions in ways that I shouldn't have. All of these things felt helpful in the moment, until I realized that they weren't quite right. These moments happen to all of us. Many people whom I've talked to about Disability say they are nervous for this precise reason. They don't want to say or do something wrong, even though they're trying to get it right like the disciples were in today's scripture.

These moments are called benevolent ableism, the good-natured attempt that doesn't land right. Benevolent ableism could be anything from infantilizing comments to helping when someone would rather do a task themselves—an action where the intent is good but the result ends up putting the Disabled person down. For example, many people have said to me, "You don't look Blind!" and while they are trying to be nice, that takes away a piece of who I am and makes me feel like they're doubting my experience.

The problem is that people are often too scared of these moments to start caring about Disability at all. Or they are so confident that they've done the right thing that they aren't open to acknowledging that it may have been well-intentioned ableism. Very likely, everyone is guilty of benevolent ableism, myself and other Disabled activists included. Benevolent ableism isn't ideal, but once it happens, acknowledging it and then moving on is better than the alternatives of avoiding Disabled people or justifying it.

The disciples in the story name that they think the money from the perfume should have gone to the poor. But Jesus corrects them. They'd tried their best to do the right thing, and it seemed like a helpful, charitable plan. But to the people experiencing it, Jesus and the woman, the right choice was a different one. The disciples were easily corrected and then they moved on, learning something about Jesus in the process. This feels like the best reaction to benevolent ableism as well: acknowledge the mistake, accept the correction, and move on. The disciples put themselves in situations to understand those on the margins and they advocated for them. They listened to those most affected by the current situation and accepted that even though they tried, they got it wrong this time. Then they learned from it. Benevolent ableism happens, but it doesn't need to scare us or be justified by us. Instead, we can advocate, be correctable, and continue learning from books, advocates, and others, continually doing our best. It's okay if we don't always get it exactly right.

CONSIDER

1. Has someone ever done something benevolently ableist to you? Have you ever done something benevolently ableist to someone else?
2. Have you ever avoided something because you were scared of trying your best but still being ableist? How could you have handled that situation differently?
3. How would you feel if you were corrected for being benevolently ableist? Can you address those feelings now so that when it does happen, you can respond more graciously?
4. What book, podcast, or other learning opportunity can you consider adding to your life?

CONNECT

Think of a time when you were trying to help but didn't get it right. Consider what you could have done differently. Write out an apology, but avoid explaining that you thought you were in the right (even if you did). Do not send the apology (because sending it would likely also end up being benevolent ableism and bring the awkward situation back up for the person). Instead, use it as a way to address the emotions that you're feeling within yourself as you write it out.

Thursday

Anointing Difference

READ

Matthew 26:10: But Jesus, aware of this, said to them, "Why do you trouble the woman? She has performed a good service for me."

REFLECT

I find this moment in Scripture compelling. Jesus takes the side of the woman, saying she is right—this woman who did the strange, startling, confusing thing that others said was wrong. If we were sitting at a similar dinner party today, I wonder if we'd agree with the disciples that her act was inappropriate, or if we'd embrace the woman for living out what she knew to be true. I wonder if it would be different if that dinner party were happening at one of the community houses I described in the first reflection for this week. Jesus' acceptance of the woman compels me to accept others. His choice to affirm her means that the strange can be sacred, confusion can be truth, and difference can be embraced. So, for those who feel strange, confused, or different, Jesus is here with us too.

As I was considering which biblical figures to write about for this book, I chose all figures who had Disability experience. This woman, however, is not identified as Disabled in the text. Interestingly, though, she does have some distinctly Disabled experiences if we are paying attention. There are many moments, especially as she does things that may seem different, when she can be seen as connecting to the Neurodivergent community. *Neurodivergent* and *Neurotypical* are terms to describe how certain brains work, which may or may not be related to Disability identity. *Neurodivergent* is a term used broadly to encompass many people whose brains work differently from the Neurotypical "norm." Neurotypical, then, describes those who do not fall into this category and whose brains most often work the way that fits into societal expectations.

The experience of the woman in this story reminds me of many Neurodivergent folks who make choices that can be beautiful and profound but do not conform to Neurotypical societal assumptions. This experience of course extends beyond Disability and Neurodiversity. But it holds a specific weight for the Neurodivergent community, who are often judged for doing things differently in social situations just like this woman was.

In addition, the story tells of her pouring a strong-smelling ointment on Jesus. The pleasant smell likely filled the room and would have been a very strong sensory experience. Actions like stimming, fidgeting, humming, burning strong-smelling candles, and eating intensely flavored snacks are all sensory-seeking behaviors that can be more significant for Neurodivergent people. This woman also seems to acknowledge that Jesus is going to die soon by anointing him in this way. Neurodivergent folks sometimes lean into honest conversations more deeply and quickly than Neurotypical people do, and this is often emphasized in conversations about death. Many Neurotypicals will add fluffy words and avoid bringing up death, but Neurodivergent people often acknowledge death like any other fact of life. Finally, the woman in this story never speaks but instead enacts this sensory and embodied way of honoring Christ. Others may honor him with their words, but she uses other forms of communication to show what she knows to be true: his approaching death and the respect that he deserves.

Many theologians speculate that this woman is Mary, the sister of Martha and Lazarus, because in the gospel of John, this story names that Mary as the woman anointing Jesus. Mary's other moments throughout Scripture also demonstrate powerful advocacy and unexpected behavior (for example, sitting at Jesus' feet instead of helping prepare the meal), which continue to relate to the actions of Neurodivergent people.

Of course, the Neurodivergent experiences I name here are at times common in many people, and sometimes even the opposite of a Neurodivergent person's experience. But broadly, the experiences of advocacy, sensory seeking, nonverbal communication, honesty about death, and unexpected social behavior relate strongly to the Neurodivergent community. Regardless of whether this woman falls into that category, Jesus, here, is clearly accepting of these types of actions that are often true of the Neurodivergent community. When we are at dinner parties or other gatherings today, I pray that we are able to extend the same acceptance and honor that Jesus does, knowing that even and especially when people are different, they are sacred.

CONSIDER

1. Does this connection between this woman and the Neurodivergent community surprise you? What is startling or uncomfortable about the connection? What feels good and right about it?
2. Have you ever had this experience of doing something differently in a social situation, whether or not you're Neurodivergent? How does Jesus' response to the woman feel in relation to your experience?
3. If you were at a dinner party today and encountered someone who was sensory-seeking, speaking too honestly, communicating nonverbally, or doing anything else similar to the woman

in this passage, how would you react? How could you help shape your and others' reactions so they are more Christlike and honor the sacredness of difference?

CONNECT

Think of something you do differently. It could be something about how you talk, act, write, joke, cook, or anything else that feels different from what others expect. Right now, take a moment to say aloud what it is and name it as beautiful. For example, "I walk with a limp and that's beautiful," or "I only like country music and that's beautiful." Make the choice today to do whatever it is boldly and to welcome God's embrace.

Friday

Anointing the Banquet Table

READ

Matthew 26:11: For you always have the poor with you, but you will not always have me.

REFLECT

This response from Jesus brings to mind another scripture passage with similar words from Christ. In Luke 14:13–14, Jesus says, "But when you give a banquet, invite the poor, the crippled, the lame, and the blind. And you will be blessed because they cannot repay you, for you will be repaid at the resurrection of the righteous." In our scripture today, Jesus says that the poor will always be among us, and he shares what to do with that information: to live alongside and in community with them. Jesus then describes this banquet in even more detail, naming that this is what the kingdom of heaven is like.

Amy Kenny is a theologian who combines church practice with Disability Justice in her powerful book *My Body Is Not a Prayer Request*. In a chapter titled "Disabled Church," she dives into this banquet theology. She names that we are all called to set the table now for this banquet that will be the full kingdom of God by including Disabled people in our churches and lives like they are in this story. Amy Kenny uses the metaphor of appetizers for the banquet. She says these appetizers are moments like when her friend started a book club to learn more about Disability or texted before an event to make sure that she would get the access she needed without her having to do the advocacy work. She describes other appetizers, like people apologizing and correcting ableist language, celebrating and decorating her mobility aides, and creating "crip spaces" that understand her experience. Kenny shares that these little moments of divine care and community do not sustain her forever, but they are a meaningful taste of the inclusive and loving banquet to come.[14]

I've experienced many of these banquet appetizer moments too. One in particular comes to mind. Several years ago, I spent a few months at a church leading a course on Disability Justice and theology for parishioners. Throughout those few weeks, a core group of people continued coming and eventually formed a group chat. Many of them were Disabled, but others were just choosing to center Disabled lives and justice. It has now been almost five years since that group chat started, and this last week alone we celebrated a win for one of our friends who got access to a mobility aide she needed and sent financial support to another who was in a housing crisis. Every few weeks, one of the members checks in to ask what our Disability wins are that week and others send questions or challenges and ask for advice. This is an accessible, supportive community that centers Disability and holds space for all of who we are. It is not the whole world or even that whole church accepting Disabled people, but it's an appetizer of the love, community, and justice that we could find at the banquet in the kingdom of God.

Amy Kenny's words are a reminder that everyone is invited to the banquet, even those who feel different or unexpected like in the dinner we've been reading about this week, and even those whom we'd rather not be at a table with. But it is not our job to choose who comes, it's our job to set the table and prepare the appetizers. It's our job to live out the inclusion and justice we hope to find at that final banquet table.

CONSIDER

1. What are some appetizers to the banquet that you've experienced? What are some appetizers to the banquet that you've helped create?
2. How can you work toward setting the table and making appetizers for the banquet with acts of inclusion and love in your life?

CONNECT

Today, make it a point to talk with someone you see every day but rarely talk to, especially someone who may be different from you. Talk to them about the weather, your work, or their day—just a simple conversation to let them know you acknowledge them. Remember that there is a spot for them at the banquet table too.

Saturday

Anointed Before It's Too Late

READ

Matthew 26:12–13: By pouring this ointment on my body she has prepared me for burial. Truly I tell you, wherever this good news is proclaimed in the whole world, what she has done will be told in remembrance of her.

REFLECT

"Do this in remembrance of me" are some of Jesus' most repeated words, spoken each time the Lord's Supper, or communion, is served. Jesus' words here mirror that as he says, "What she has done will be told in remembrance of her." The woman's story was important enough for Jesus to tie it to the memory of his life. That shows the incredible weight that even Jesus gives to this moment. It is worth remembering and worth holding together with the gospel.

The story of this woman centers around honoring Jesus' body. Jesus specifically notes that it's worth remembering this honoring of his flesh and bones. So often, church spaces put an emphasis on the spiritual life and soul while pushing away from honoring or even thinking about our bodies, especially when it comes to Jesus. Jesus' body is often turned into a spiritualized matter, and his embodied presence is often secondary. But here, Jesus tells us to remember the honoring of his physical body as part of the good news. He says we are to tell this "in remembrance of her" just as he does when he takes the bread and wine and offers himself to his community.

In the Lord's Supper, Jesus also honors his body in a powerful way, and that honoring continues today as many churches eat the bread, drink the wine, and regularly repeat his words. "Here is my body, given for you" and "Here is my blood of the covenant, poured out for the forgiveness of sins" accompany his "Do this in remembrance of me" (see Matthew 26:26–28; 1 Corinthians 11:23–26). These are not comments about Jesus' spirit or his holiness; they are his body and blood, flesh and bones. This is Jesus honoring his own body and allowing us to do the same. This woman in Scripture knew even before he died that his body was to be honored. Jesus reflected that as he passed around the bread and the cup, sharing and honoring his body and blood among the disciples. They may not have understood, but he and this woman both knew that bodies are important, and they are meant to be honored, not just in death, but all throughout life.

Our culture puts pressure, strain, and often hatred on bodies, wishing that they'd be more productive, invincible, beautiful, and more. We do this especially to bodies that are on the margins and don't match those ideals. But what if we listened to Jesus and remembered these moments of honoring bodies?

A church I attend has a beautiful way of doing this. They have pushed the pews to the sides of the sanctuary, creating a circle where the pews face one another. This is lovely during the music and the sermon, as you can see those worshiping with you. It is perhaps the most meaningful, though, when it comes time for the Lord's Supper. We all watch the bread and wine move toward the congregation, and then watch those walking through the circle to receive. We get to see one another's faces, hear one another's voices, feel one another's presence as we take communion.

In this way, bodies are sacred and honored as they are. Our faith becomes more embodied, and we recognize the holiness of one another's bodies as each person takes from the bread and cup. In Scripture, the disciples would have waited until Jesus was dead to honor his body in this way, but this woman honors Christ's body before. As we move toward the end of Lent, contemplating our finitude, I pray we can learn to honor our bodies and those that surround us before it's too late.

CONSIDER

1. Do you put more emphasis on the body or the soul? Why?
2. What would it mean to honor your body well? What would it mean to honor the bodies of those around you? How can you do this in your daily life?
3. What piece of this story that Jesus tells us to remember do you most want to hold on to?

CONNECT

Do something in memory of someone you love who has passed (light a candle, write a poem, reflect on a walk, have a conversation, etc.). Then do a similar practice to honor yourself and the people in your life now in the same way (light a second candle, write a second poem, walk the other way, have a second conversation).

Palm Sunday

God who has dinner parties,

Make space at the table for us. Help us make space at the table for others. It is startling and inspiring to watch you sit down at the house of a Leper and accept a woman who does the unexpected. Help us remember that these are the people at your table. Help us have this diversity at our tables too. Share with us, God, appetizers for the banquet, little moments of hope for love, justice, and joy. Allow us to have those moments in our lives and help us create those moments for others. Thank you for accepting all the difference and diversity in your group of disciples and friends at this banquet table. Thank you for accepting all the difference and diversity in us. Help us accept ourselves and others, even and especially when we are different from one another and different from what people expect. You know the importance of this difference. You know the importance of our unique bodies and minds. Thank you for honoring your body and your blood at many different tables so that we know it is okay to honor ours. Let the unexpected be sacred. Let difference bring community. Let our bodies and minds be cherished for all of who we are. Keep extending the table.

Amen.

Breathe in: We are unexpected
Breathe out: We are sacred

Breathe in: Extend the table, God,
Breathe out: Help us welcome everyone

Breathe in: Meet us, God,
Breathe out: At the banquet table

Breathe in: Fill our tables
Breathe out: With diverse community

Breathe in: Welcome all of us
Breathe out: We are different, we are good

Holy Week and Easter

Resurrected

EXCERPTS FROM THE
GOSPEL OF MATTHEW

Monday

Resurrecting Our Joy

READ

Matthew 21:6–11: The disciples went and did as Jesus had directed them; they brought the donkey and the colt and put their cloaks on them, and he sat on them. A very large crowd spread their cloaks on the road, and others cut branches from the trees and spread them on the road. The crowds that went ahead of him and that followed were shouting,

"Hosanna to the Son of David!
Blessed is the one who comes in the name of the Lord!
Hosanna in the highest heaven!"

When he entered Jerusalem, the whole city was in turmoil, asking, "Who is this?" The crowds were saying, "This is the prophet Jesus from Nazareth in Galilee."

REFLECT

I remember the crowd gathered in our parking lot, marching through the balloon arches with signs and banners, spreading out their coats and sitting on the ground, watching and listening intently to the speakers. I had experienced a few parades in my life before, but nothing quite like this. This moment was the biggest project I'd ever attempted, planning the city of Durham's first Disability Pride Parade with a few neighbors and friends. We expected to have a good turnout, but nothing could have prepared us for over six hundred people at our first event. Over forty volunteers, twenty-five organizations marching or tabling, seven speakers, an amazing band, and food and coffee venders, all created and led by Disabled people. Instead of mingling like I expected folks to, everyone spread out their jackets and blankets and sat on the asphalt of the parking lot to listen or watch the sign language interpreter as the speakers shared why they were proud to be Disabled. People had flown in for the event. They heard about it on the radio and turned their cars around to attend. They saw posters around the city and posts on social media and hadn't realized that there was a space like this for them. It was such a beautiful moment of a crowd coming together to celebrate the identity, truth, and community that we had found.

Many people think of parades and marches when Palm Sunday comes around. The crowds ushering people in, cheering and crying out as Jesus walked by, and waving branches like signs are all similar to parades now. But there are more meaningful similarities too. In the United States, Disability Pride Month celebrates the passage of the Americans with Disabilities Act on July 26, and parades take place around the country that weekend. These events create community, honor identities and truth, and celebrate the powerful work already happening. Durham was the perfect representation of this because there was so much Disability community ready to come together. Many nonprofits and churches had learned about what it means to honor Disabled identities, and so much work had already been done to create employment, housing, leisure, and more for Disabled people. This parade brought them all together to recognize and celebrate it.

These reasons for marching in our parade seem to mirror some of the feeling on that first Palm Sunday. People were ready to honor the truth of who Jesus was. They cried out, "Hosanna! Save us!"—recognizing his identity and what he brought. They celebrated this truth because they knew Jesus had been doing the work of restoring people to community, opening up space at the table, and inviting in more and more people throughout his ministry. This was a moment when all those affected by Jesus' invitation got to celebrate it. Some interpreters note how the people's welcome was even a deeply political act, since many believed they were welcoming a king who would overturn the empire.

But they waved their palm fronds and shouted not because they thought it would be fun, to draw attention to themselves, or even necessarily to make much of a political statement. Instead, they gathered to name the truth in community, that Jesus had come to save. Disability Pride Parades across the country do the same. Are they political, attention-drawing, and fun? Yes. More importantly, though, they are a space to honor the truth of the amazing community and the work that has been done. On that summer day in Durham, North Carolina, when everyone paused to sit and take in the speakers, I found all of those things and more. In that moment, I found God, and I learned about how we are saved through our community and love like this.

CONSIDER

1. What other similarities do you recognize between these parades and Palm Sunday celebrations?
2. Where do you think Jesus is most clearly showing up in parades like this today? Where else do you think Jesus is showing up in similar ways?
3. What truths, identities, work, or communities do you find yourself wanting to honor this Holy Week?

CONNECT

Buy, draw, or print out a palm frond or a flag like the Disability Pride flag. Images are available online to print, order, or help you draw one. Hang up that leaf or flag in your space to remind you to celebrate the truth of Jesus and to celebrate the truth, identity, and community that come with Disability and other marginalized identities.

Tuesday

No Hope for Resurrection

READ

Matthew 27:1–2, 11–14, 22–26: When morning came, all the chief priests and the elders of the people conferred together against Jesus in order to bring about his death. They bound him, led him away, and handed him over to Pilate the governor. . . .

Now Jesus stood before the governor, and the governor asked him, "Are you the king of the Jews?" Jesus said, "You say so." But when he was accused by the chief priests and elders, he did not answer. Then Pilate said to him, "Do you not hear how many accusations they make against you?" But he gave him no answer, not even to a single charge, so that the governor was greatly amazed. . . .

Pilate said to [the crowd], "Then what should I do with Jesus who is called the Messiah?" All of them said, "Let him be crucified!" Then he asked, "Why, what evil has he done?" But they shouted all the more, "Let him be crucified!"

So when Pilate saw that he could do nothing but rather that a riot was beginning, he took some water and washed his hands before the crowd, saying, "I am innocent of this man's blood; see to it yourselves." Then the people as a whole answered, "His blood be on us and on our children!" So he released Barabbas for them, and after flogging Jesus he handed him over to be crucified.

REFLECT

Today is a moment to dive into the heaviness of all that Holy Week brings. Easter coming promises hope of resurrection, but it is not here yet. First, we must move through the pain that we find in the story of our Savior, and only then can we understand the sweetness of the truth in resurrection. Today is going to be filled with heavy, maybe triggering, moments of Jesus' story of death and the stories of Disabled people's mourning and pain as well.

As we start this journey of Holy Week, we remember how Jesus was condemned not only by Roman authorities but also by the religious leaders, including his followers and friends. As we remember the ways that our God was condemned, let us also bring to mind the condemnation of the Disabled community, especially by religious spaces. Throughout history, the church has denied Disabled people baptism and communion, refused to participate in civil rights laws to make churches accessible, and used theology that dehumanizes. Disabled people are often viewed by the church as a result of the fall after creation, as a "punishment" from God or as something "broken" that God must "fix," rather than as people who are created fearfully and wonderfully in God's own image.

In the United States, Disabled people's legal rights have been denied by the church repeatedly, especially through churches' refusal to participate in the Americans with Disabilities Act. Some Christian leaders protested the ADA because they didn't want to make changes to their historic buildings and they were committed to denying support to those with HIV and AIDS, whom the law included in its protections. These church leaders successfully sought for churches be exempt from the ADA. So even today, churches have no legal requirement to be accessible, inclusive, or anti-discriminatory toward Disabled people.[15]

When Jesus was condemned to death, the world lost a significant piece of God's embodied presence. If the church continues to condemn Disabled people, it loses a piece of who God is as well. The people in Jesus' time were pushing against hope. They were fighting for his death and pushing his love and justice away. Those who continue to pursue and accept ableist beliefs are denying the hope and resurrection of Jesus as well. Ableism denies hope. It fights for death.

Every year, the Disabled community honors Disabled Day of Mourning on March 1. As we learned before, it acknowledges the mourning in our community for those who have been harmed or killed by caretakers and parents. Caretaker violence reveals where this fight for death and push against hope is clear, but the gathering of Disabled people to remember the lives lost is a reminder of the resurrection hope of Jesus. Today we read about Jesus being killed at the hands of a government. We know that not all governments protect people from harm, but ideally, a government should support its people. These Disabled people were killed by those who were supposed to provide them support as well.

In the past few years, hundreds of people have been killed by caretakers through the violence of intentional overmedicating, suffocation, fire, and more.[16] March 1, Disabled Day of Mourning, allows us to recognize this and celebrate the Disabled community who still fights for love and justice. Just as Holy Week invites us to hold the heaviness of Jesus' death, today, let us hold the heaviness of each of these painful realities for the Disabled community. We know, as we read Scripture and as we think about the loss in the Disabled community, that there is hope even in this radical sadness and loss. Even in this pain, when it seems like there is no hope of resurrection, we believe in a God and a humanity that resurrects with love.

CONSIDER

1. How are you feeling after the heaviness of this reflection? How can you care for your body in those feelings?
2. Before reading this reflection, were you familiar with Disabled Day of Mourning? If not, would you have the capacity to learn more by finding the affiliated website and reading through some of the names and stories? Or does that feel like too much?
3. Where can you find hope even when it feels like there is none? Even if it's in the smallest of actions or moments?

CONNECT

Wear black today—as noticeable as a whole black outfit or as private as just a black hair tie—and when you remember what you are wearing, think about the Disabled people who have been killed by caretaker violence and think about Jesus' death in solidarity with the marginalized.

Wednesday

Resurrecting Ideas of Care

READ

Matthew 27:32: As they went out, they came upon a man from Cyrene named Simon; they compelled this man to carry his cross.

REFLECT

This image of Simon helping Jesus is a picture of what it means to be a friend, an ally, a follower of Christ. By carrying this burden alongside Jesus, Simon is doing something holy. He is living into the interdependent, communal life that Jesus repeatedly calls us to, even through one of the hardest moments one could imagine. Of course, in this passage Simon is compelled, even forced, to share this burden, but this also paints an accurate picture of how we are all intertwined. Even when something is not directly our own, we are compelled to experience it together. Simon was likely hurting just from knowing that Christ was being hurt, and this was a way that he physically recognized that and helped Christ not to have to feel all of it alone. This sharing of hardship, just as they may have shared life's joys and journeys, is a core piece of what Christianity calls us to. We are called to be with and for one another, just as Jesus in his life and even death was with and for all of us.

Another story of interdependence is shown in this same moment in some Catholic and other Christian traditions. These churches follow Stations of the Cross on Good Friday (or during Holy Week and Lent more broadly). Stations of the Cross are a way for churches to gather and process Christ's journey to death by moving through twelve stations of art and reflection that represent the different moments of his crucifixion story. In some Stations of the Cross, Simon's act of care is followed shortly by care from a woman named Veronica. Veronica, while not mentioned in Scripture, is a saint in the Catholic Church who is believed by some to have been present at the crucifixion.

In Veronica's story, she approaches Jesus and wipes the sweat off his face as he carries his cross. When she takes back the cloth that she wiped him with, she notices that his face left an imprint. It is an image of himself, though slightly disfigured. This act of care represents the ways that when we dive into caring for one another, we glimpse the image of God. It may be challenging, confusing, or messy to attempt to care well for our neighbor, but God's image is there, even if it's disfigured. God's image is there even if we don't always find it with complete clarity.

Disability Justice centers the idea of interdependence and brings that view of community uniquely to the church. Author and activist Leah Lakshmi Piepzna-Samarasinha describes this sort of interdependence as "shift[ing] ideas of access and care (whether it's a disability, childcare, economic access or many more) from an individual chore, an unfortunate cost of having an unfortunate body, to a collective responsibility that is maybe even deeply joyful."[17] This sort of care shows up everywhere in Disability history and justice. It's found in the 504 Sit-in and Capitol Crawl. It's found in Disability Pride Parades and Disabled housing. It's found in moments of friends, families, neighbors, church members, and strangers learning to care for each other well and accept all of what it means to be embodied. This care is hard and messy. The image of God it leaves can be distorted, and we are often left carrying the weight of others' challenges. But it is also reflective of God's image. It is also what we are called and compelled to do. It is also maybe even deeply joyful.

CONSIDER

1. Have you ever been cared for in a way that felt communal and maybe even deeply joyful? Have you ever cared for someone else in that way? Have you ever experienced or given care in a way that made you feel like you were left carrying others' weight? Or holding the image of God, even if it was disfigured?
2. Does the idea of this type of collective care work feel exciting or daunting? Challenging, necessary, impossible, joyful? Why?

CONNECT

Consider the story of Veronica washing the face of Jesus. Wash your own face with a cloth like Veronica wiped Jesus' face. When you take the cloth off your face, hold it in your hand and remember that you are made in the image of God.

Maundy Thursday

Broken Body Resurrected

READ

Matthew 26:26–29: While they were eating, Jesus took a loaf of bread, and after blessing it he broke it, gave it to the disciples, and said, "Take, eat; this is my body." Then he took a cup, and after giving thanks he gave it to them, saying, "Drink from it, all of you, for this is my blood of the covenant, which is poured out for many for the forgiveness of sins. I tell you, I will never again drink of this fruit of the vine until that day when I drink it new with you in my Father's kingdom."

REFLECT

For weeks, we have been reflecting on how God loves, changes, and reflects God's own image in our bodies. Maybe the most prominent expression of all of these takes place in the Lord's Supper. Especially on Maundy Thursday, the day that the church calendar celebrates this scripture and the moment when Jesus offers the first communion, it is important for us to consider the Lord's Supper and its mystery and meaning.

The Lord's Supper is a fundamental changing of our bodies in a way that pulls us closer to God. We are invited to the table to participate in the changing of Christ's body through life, death, and resurrection. We are pulled into Christ's own breaking, changing, and resurrecting. We are welcomed in to God doing that work in us as well. The Lord's Supper links us with Christ and Christians over centuries and spaces. Our bodies become linked in God's image, to Jesus' body, and to one another in the taking of the bread and the cup.

This is the climactic moment of the liturgy, the momentary fulfillment of the hope that all will be welcomed to the table. Jesus says to do this every time we eat and drink of it. This is a continuous promise that people are welcome, included, and loved, not just this once, but every time we take communion. It is especially beautiful to reflect on this moment of welcome knowing that it is with the disciples, a messy, diverse group of people who started off as everything from religious leaders and fishermen to tax collectors and carpenters. Jesus even notes that there is someone at the table who will betray him. Yet everyone is still welcome.

As the Lord's Supper invites us into community with God and with others, it also invites us into a new understanding of our own bodies. As we take and eat, we mirror the act of eating that we do every day. When we eat, it is often to take in sustenance that will keep us healthy and keep our bodies nourished, strong, and fit. While this goal of health is of course important, it also often gets wrapped up in ableist ideals of wholeness. People understand those who have healthy, strong, and fit bodies to be whole, and those who have Disabled, sick, or unhealthy bodies or minds to be broken or lacking. In the Lord's Supper, we are pushing against this connection between health and wholeness, recognizing the elements as the broken body and blood of Christ that makes us whole. This taking in of brokenness in order to truly make us whole in our connection with God, others, and ourselves creates a new, more inclusive understanding of wholeness.

Disability theology finds great resonance in the Lord's Supper, in its reimagining of wholeness, commitment to inclusion, and welcoming of interdependence with God, God's image, and the community around us today and from centuries past. Welcoming Disability theology into the church is helpful not only to create inclusion, but to more fully understand what God is doing in the world and in our bodies. The Lord's Supper can be understood through a Disability theology lens that allows for even more truth, love, community, and wholeness to be welcomed into our bodies and our churches.

CONSIDER

1. What does the Lord's Supper mean for you? If you take communion, what do you think about as you take it? What would it mean for you to let it be a moment of change in your body and life?
2. Does this reflection make you think differently about the Lord's Supper? What felt exciting? What felt unsettling? Why? What other aspects of communion do you think could be included in this reflection?
3. Do health and wholeness seem related to you? What else does wholeness include that is broader than health? Have you experienced health and wholeness linked in helpful or harmful ways, whether in the church or outside of it?

CONNECT

Go to your kitchen and grab some bread and juice (or the closest thing to it) from your cabinets. Hold them in your hands and reflect on the moments in church when you have taken communion. Eat and drink them, not as consecrated or special elements like in a church setting, but as an embodied way to reflect on what true communion means for you when it does happen in church, based on this reflection and your own experience with it. Think especially about how it connects you to God, community, and your own brokenness and wholeness. If the Lord's Supper is not a custom that resonates with you, consider more broadly the food in your home and how moments of cooking, eating, and sharing food reveal God's presence to you.

Good Friday

Resurrecting Identity of Jesus

READ

Matthew 27:33–54: And when they came to a place called Golgotha (which means Place of a Skull), they offered him wine to drink, mixed with gall, but when he tasted it, he would not drink it. And when they had crucified him, they divided his clothes among themselves by casting lots; then they sat down there and kept watch over him. Over his head they put the charge against him, which read, "This is Jesus, the King of the Jews."

Then two rebels were crucified with him, one on his right and one on his left. Those who passed by derided him, shaking their heads and saying, "You who would destroy the temple and build it in three days, save yourself! If you are the Son of God, come down from the cross." In the same way the chief priests also, along with the scribes and elders, were mocking him, saying, "He saved others; he cannot save himself. He is the King of Israel; let him come down from the cross now, and we will believe in him. He trusts in God; let God deliver him now, if he wants to, for he said, 'I am God's Son.'" The rebels who were crucified with him also taunted him in the same way.

From noon on, darkness came over the whole land until three in the afternoon. And about three o'clock Jesus cried with a loud voice, "Eli, Eli, lema sabachthani?" that is, "My God, my God, why have you forsaken me?" When some of the bystanders heard it, they said,

"This man is calling for Elijah." At once one of them ran and got a sponge, filled it with sour wine, put it on a stick, and gave it to him to drink. But the others said, "Wait, let us see whether Elijah will come to save him." Then Jesus cried again with a loud voice and breathed his last. At that moment the curtain of the temple was torn in two, from top to bottom. The earth shook, and the rocks were split. The tombs also were opened, and many bodies of the saints who had fallen asleep were raised. After his resurrection they came out of the tombs and entered the holy city and appeared to many. Now when the centurion and those with him, who were keeping watch over Jesus, saw the earthquake and what took place, they were terrified and said, "Truly this man was God's Son!"

REFLECT

Good Friday is the day when we recognize Christ's death. All of Lent has been leading up to these few days, giving us a space to wait on, mourn, and honor Jesus before we are able to move into the hope of resurrection.

Throughout Holy Week, and all of Lent, we have reflected on the challenges and celebrations of the Disabled community. We have celebrated the moments of Disability history, the power of Disabled community, and the hope in Disability theology that the entire church can grow from. These hopeful moments could not come without a recognition of the challenges as well. In the past few weeks, we've recognized those who have died at the hands of caretakers, the pain that discrimination in the law and community has caused, and the ways that the church has been complacent or encouraging in the face of ableism. In the weight of this harsh reality, we are all called to hold this heaviness and offer help. That heaviness would weigh us down without the hope we've found. There cannot be resurrection without death, and now, thanks to Christ, there is no death without resurrection.

We can hold the heaviness and hope together, even on the bleakest of days. Christ's death is one of the places where that heaviness is most present—and yet radical hope somehow still exists. For the Disabled community this is particularly true. As Jesus was pierced by nails and a sword, he received the injuries that appear in the resurrection story. His hands and his feet and his side were brutally wounded. In this moment, Christ became the Disabled God.

In *The Disabled God*, a groundbreaking book of Disability theology, theologian Nancy Eiesland writes that "in presenting his impaired body to his startled friends, the resurrected Jesus is revealed as the disabled God."[18] After his resurrection, Christ is raised with the wounds he received on the cross. These wounds in Christ post-resurrection become not only a way that his friends identify him, but also a reminder of his identity for all of us for centuries after. He is God, identified by his Disability. Most importantly, he was Disabled even after his resurrection, showing that Disabled people also have a place in the post-resurrection community of God. The moment when Jesus is nailed to the cross was the painful birthplace of the Disabled God.

In Scripture, the disciple Thomas is credited with wanting to touch Christ's scars when he appears after the resurrection. Many people say that this means he doubted, but in some ways, Thomas's request is the opposite of doubt. It is the acceptance of all the truth. That Jesus is not his full self without his full story, including the story of the cross. Thomas asks to feel Jesus' hands and side, and in this moment after resurrection, Jesus' full story is recognized. All of who Christ is was honored in that moment. Thomas and others held the heaviness and the hope together. They held the heaviness of

Christ's death, his pain, the harm from government and society, and his community's great loss alongside Christ's understanding of and identifying with the Disabled experience and the Disciples' faith in of all of who Christ was. There is so much pain, and so much hope. So much power in Disability identity, and so much ableist harm. So much death, and so much resurrection.

CONSIDER

1. Have you heard of the concept of the Disabled God? What does it mean that Christ's wounds are still there even after resurrection? What difference does it make that they are there and that he is identified by them?
2. What are you mourning on this Good Friday? How can you ask God to come alongside you in that? How can you hold heaviness and hope?

CONNECT

As you consider the concept of Christ as the Disabled God, write out a prayer directly addressed to the Disabled God. Pray for yourself, the church, and the Disabled community, paying specific attention to what God may understand, experience, or encapsulate as the Disabled God, rather than if Christ had resurrected without wounds. Consider Jesus currently ascended to the right side of God as the Disabled God, making space in the post-resurrection kingdom for Disabled people and all bodies. Also consider the moment when Thomas asks to feel Christ's wounds. Think of a question you have for God and write it into the prayer. Then pray your prayer aloud or in your mind in a way that cements it for you.

Holy Saturday

Waiting for Resurrection

READ

Matthew 27:57–66: When it was evening, there came a rich man from Arimathea named Joseph, who also was himself a disciple of Jesus. He went to Pilate and asked for the body of Jesus; then Pilate ordered it to be given to him. So Joseph took the body and wrapped it in a clean linen cloth and laid it in his new tomb, which he had hewn in the rock. He then rolled a great stone to the door of the tomb and went away. Mary Magdalene and the other Mary were there, sitting opposite the tomb.

The next day, that is, after the day of Preparation, the chief priests and the Pharisees gathered before Pilate and said, "Sir, we remember what that impostor said while he was still alive, 'After three days I will rise again.' Therefore command the tomb to be made secure until the third day; otherwise, his disciples may go and steal him away and tell the people, 'He has been raised from the dead,' and the last deception would be worse than the first." Pilate said to them, "You have a guard of soldiers; go, make it as secure as you can." So they went with the guard and made the tomb secure by sealing the stone.

REFLECT

Holy Saturday is a unique day in the church calendar. It is full of so many emotions. It is marked by confusion and mystery. It wraps us in a hug and says that it can hold all of our pain. If it can hold the death of God, it can hold our pains and challenges as well. If there can still be a glimmer of hope in Holy Saturday, then hope can exist, even in the smallest of ways, even on the hardest of days. Holy Saturday is the end of all of the waiting of Lent; it is the rock bottom of faith; it is the death before resurrection, when resurrection seems impossible. Holy Saturday gives us space to grieve without silly platitudes and optimistic denial. It embraces us, not to say that it will be okay, but to say "I am here," "God was here," and "God is, even, here." It is solidarity, not avoidance; communion, not denial; empathy, not pity. Holy Saturday is a space for us, all of us, at our lowest.

Holy Saturday is the day that most fully welcomes our "already, not yet" faith. Already God is in the world, but God is not yet accepted. Already there is hope, but it is not yet realized. Already justice and love have come, but not yet are they prevailing. Remember the 504 Sit-in. How the activists lived out the anti-discrimination they wanted for the world around them as they fought for it. They were living in this already-and-not-yet reality. Already people know Disabled people deserve love and justice, but not yet have they prevailed. Already we have practiced anti-discrimination, but not yet is it the way of the world. Already Disabled people are leading a revolution and changing hearts, but not yet has it changed the whole world.

We are living in the already and not yet of God's presence here, of love and justice for all people, and of hope for ourselves and our communities, the Disabled community, and the world. As we welcome Holy Saturday's heaviness and hope, I pray that we become more open to this already-and-not-yet reality. May we strive like they did in the sit-in to live out the love we wish for the world. May we welcome all the heaviness that we hold and still believe there is a glimpse of hope for us somewhere. May we accept the already and not yet, knowing that God is there too. Even on the Holy Saturdays of our lives, even in the already and not yet, may we remember Emmanuel, God is with us.

CONSIDER

1. This Holy Saturday, are you holding more hope or more heaviness? Do you feel God in the midst of it?
2. What circumstances in your life feel most connected to the already and not yet? How can you hold both the hope and heaviness together as you move through them?
3. What are you taking away from this devotional and this Lenten season? How has it helped you live better in the already-and-not-yet world?

CONNECT

As we sit in this Holy Saturday, mourning the death of Jesus, take a moment of silence. Consider the aspects of your life that feel like they are waiting for resurrection. Take this time of silence to consider your own already and not yet and how you can be open to holding both the heaviness and hope. Finish the moment of silence acknowledging that God is there in all of it, even on Holy Saturday as you wait for Easter.

Easter Sunday

God who is identified by Disability,

This moment shows us that you are there in it all. You were there as the people waved palm fronds and yelled, "Hosanna! Save us!" and you were there at the Disability Pride Parade as people waved their signs and celebrated our community and identity. You were there when Simon carried your cross and Veronica washed your face, being cared for by your community, and you are there when we have moments of care and interdependence that leave us with a messy, holy picture of who you are. You were there even in death, even as you died on a cross, and you are there when Disabled people die at the hands of caretakers and when communities kill the hope of love with ableism. You were there on Holy Saturday even when no one knew it, and you are there on our hard days, holding the pain with us even when we cannot find you. You were there in the resurrection, in the hope of Easter morning, and you are there in our impossible hope for new life now. You were there after resurrection as they identified you by your wounds, by your Disability, and you are there to welcome all of the truth of our identities as well.

You are there so that we can have hope on this Easter and always. Hope in Christ's resurrection, in the Disabled God. Hope in interdependence, in people learning and making change. Hope in theologians like Nancy Eiesland, in activists like Judy Heumann and Leah Lakshmi Piepzna-Samarasinha. Hope in the little moments of

Disabled joy and pride we find in this work. Hope in each other, and hope in the body of Christ.

Amen.

Breathe in: This Easter,
Breathe out: resurrect my hope

Breathe in: We are made whole
Breathe out: Through love and care

Breathe in: This is my body
Breathe out: This is my blood

Breathe in: You were there
Breathe out: In it all

Breathe in: Emmanuel
Breathe out: God with us

Acknowledgments

Just as so much of Disability Justice and theology hinge on interdependence, this book would not exist without the wisdom, care, and support of so many. I am deeply grateful to the brilliant minds, kind friends, fierce advocates, and generous coffee shops (Everlou specifically) that have shaped both this work and my understanding of the Disability Justice and theology shared within it.

First, I would like to extend my gratitude to the amazing team of people who have been working on this book alongside me, starting with my fantastic editor Sara Versluis. Sara, thank you for making this process enjoyable, accessible, and successful. Your edits, support, and direction helped to make this book what it is, and I will forever be grateful for that. Thank you, as well, to the rest of the Herald Press team, including those who designed this absolutely beautiful cover that features Disability Pride so prominently, and the media team who worked to get this book into the hands and hearts of many. I am deeply grateful to have had the opportunity to write for Herald Press, a publishing company that has so consistently been committed to justice work and theology that liberates and loves.

In addition, this book would not have been possible without the professors who mentored me through the writing of it—Jerusha Neal and Sarah Barton. The structure, theology, stories, and prayers in this book formed as I took independent study classes with them. I am deeply grateful, Sarah, for the ways that you continuously support my work as a Disability theologian and share your own wisdom and experience with me, especially as I developed the prayers in this book. Jerusha, I am grateful for the ways that you sat with me to form the outline of the book and theology of each devotion. Your wisdom and voice helped me find my own, and I am very grateful for that.

I would also like to extend a huge thank you to the friends and family who worked on the dreaming, writing, and editing of this book with me. Rebekah Schultz, my amazing partner and best friend, thank you for reading, talking, thinking, creating, and theologizing alongside me through this whole process and through life. You have taught me how to find love, justice, and goodness everywhere I go and have encouraged me to let it shine through my words in this book and beyond. Thank you to my mom Valerie Christian and my dad Dan Tricarico for reading the first draft of this book and all my writing for many, many years. Thank you for encouraging me from elementary school on that being an author was a possibility and continuing to support and love me in all I set out to do. Tessa Tricarico, thank you for being not just a sister but a best friend who helps me brainstorm all my ideas and encourages me to put myself out there even when I hesitate.

Thank you to Camryn Marble and Jennifer Ingold Asbill for also reading the entire rough draft and editing it alongside me. Cami, the Disability Justice you live out makes this book and my life better. The conversations we have entertain, sustain, and educate me always, and I'm grateful for you. Jennifer, thank you for letting me lean on your powerful thoughts of theology, justice, and love. You are a gift, and I am grateful for your help with this manuscript and your friendship.

Before this book was a book, it was a Disability Justice Stations of the Cross program. Laura Steed Lorino, thank you from the bottom of my heart for the incredible support you gave me in the years I've worked with you and beyond to help me develop these stations, fine-tune my Disability theology, and put my call into practice. Thank you for believing in me and helping me make my impact on the world. Melissa Florer-Bixler, thank you for reading it as Stations of the Cross and finding something in it that was worth sharing with your publisher friends, which helped me believe it was worth developing further as well.

The theology in this book also could not have happened without countless hours of conversations (some of which are mentioned in the devotions) with professors and pastors who have become dear friends. At Duke Divinity, in addition to Jerusha and Sarah, I would like to thank Christine Parton Burkett for helping me expand my understanding of Scripture in creative ways, some of which appear in the "connect" sections of this devotional; Wylin Wilson for helping develop my understanding of a God who liberates and loves the oppressed; and Sangwoo Kim for expanding my view of prayer and supporting my calling in ministry.

From Point Loma Nazarene University, I want to first thank Melissa Tucker for being my pastor, professor, mentor, and most of all, friend. Your friendship has impacted me in ways that I cannot even articulate. You have helped me feel comfortable in prayer, find my path as a minister, and name my passion for justice and truth-telling, as well as been a trusted and treasured friend. Thank you to Heather Ross, Rob Thompson, and Katie Manning for being my honors project committee. That project was the basis for the theology in this book, and conversations with all three of you helped me get to the point where I'm at both theologically and personally. Thank you for helping me develop a theology that makes space for me and my community in everything from our classes and honors discussions to long meetings in your offices or on Zoom to the friendship you've extended to me beyond my time in your class. Thank you also to Rebecca Laird for introducing me to *The Disabled God* and the framework of Disability theologians who have come before me. Thank you to Stephanie Smith-Matthews, John Manning, and Kara Lyons-Pardue for developing my ability to interpret Scripture and find its loving and liberating nature. Thank you to Denise Necoechea for introducing me to Disability Rights and Justice leaders and concepts. The knowledge you gave me will never stop impacting my life and work, and this book could not have happened without it. And lastly, thank you to Dee Kelley and Mark Maddix for teaching me much about theology, including but not limited to what it means to truly live in a way that loves all your neighbors, no matter the cost.

I would also like to thank Evan Milbern for his friendship and shared joy and passion for Disability Justice leadership. Thank you to all of the YO team and the Disabled Server crew for creating spaces where I find Disabled leadership and friendship in ways I never dreamed possible. Thank you to all of Friendship House and North Street for being the Disability community I never knew I needed, Wendy Lincicome and Sloan Meek for celebrating Disability Pride with me, and Jenn Barnes, Kim Edwards, and many, many others for being my great friends. Thank you to the community I've formed on Instagram @blind_person_in_area because Disability Justice is so present online, and your support and activity has been a joy to facilitate. Thank you to the other Disability Justice social media leaders whom I have learned so much from, including how to live proudly and take up space. Thank you to the Duke Memorial and Wesley Memorial Church communities for being places where I feel loved and welcomed by God and friends for all of who I am. Thank you to Laurie Wevers for helping me find the places where God is showing up in my life, work, and prayer and processing through the moments when God feels far away. Thank you to the Misfits for being my friends for so long and teaching me from an early age what true inclusion looks like. Thank you to Jana Schwerdtfeger, Sue Scheffers, and Kathy Kaiser for helping me learn the ins and outs of being Blind in a way that supported my passions and helped me dream of an inclusive future for myself. Thank you to Lori Hill and Adele Buffington for mentoring me as I learned who I was and where I fit in the church—Lori for reading and attending all of my early writing and preaching, and Adele for teaching me the basics of theology—including what the word *Lent* means when I was a middle schooler (it's not from a dryer after all!). Thank you to Rachael and Donna Liebrecht for being my constant cheerleaders, confidants, and friends and for reading many, many books with me. And thank you, Nanny, for being a constant figure of support, encouragement, and love for every part of me and everything I do, even now.

Finally, thank you to the Disabled leaders I mentioned in the dedication, as well as the countless others who have paved the way for me in our collective theology, culture, justice, and pride. I am forever grateful for all of you.

Notes

1. Activist-attorney Talila A. Lewis defines ableism as "a system of assigning value to people's bodies and minds based on societally constructed ideas of normalcy, productivity, desirability, intelligence, excellence, and fitness. These constructed ideas are deeply rooted in eugenics, anti-Blackness, misogyny, colonialism, imperialism, and capitalism. This systemic oppression leads to people and society determining people's value based on their culture, age, language, appearance, religion, birth or living place, 'health/wellness,' and/or their ability to satisfactorily re/produce, 'excel' and 'behave.'" Talila A. Lewis, "Working Definition of Ableism—January 2022 Update," *TL's Blog*, January 1, 2022, https://www.talilalewis.com/blog/working-definition-of-ableism-january-2022-update.
2. Alice Wong with Leah Lakshmi Piepzna-Samarasinha and Stacey Milbern, "Episode 6: Labor, Care Work, and Disabled and Queer Femmes," October 22, 2017, in *Disability Visibility Podcast*, 28:20, transcript by Cheryl Green available at https://disabilityvisibilityproject.com/wp-content/uploads/2017/10/Labor-Care-Work-Disabled-and-Queer-Femmes.pdf.
3. See, e.g., James Cone, *The Cross and the Lynching Tree* (Orbis, 2011).
4. For one record, see "Disability Day of Mourning," https://disability-memorial.org/.
5. Eden Summerlin, "Autistic People Often Have Atypical Spiritual Practices and Experiences," *The Autisticats* (blog), July 12, 2020, https://theautisticats.weebly.com/uploads/1/2/9/6/129686841/autistic_people_often_have_atypical_spiritual_practices_and_experiences.pdf.
6. Lois Curtis and Lee Sanders, "Lois Curtis on Life after Olmstead," *Impact* 28, no. 1 (Winter 2015), https://publications.ici.umn.edu/impact/28-1/lois-curtis-on-life-after-olmstead.
7. Stella Young, "I'm Not Your Inspiration, Thank You Very Much," TEDxSydney, 9:02, April 2014, https://www.ted.com/talks/stella_young_i_m_not_your_inspiration_thank_you_very_much/transcript.
8. Dan Thompson, "Ugly Laws: The History of Disability Regulation in North America," *Progress*, Spring 2011, https://www.ambest.com/directories/bestconnect/DeeGeeArticle.pdf.

9. "Worth Repeating: Ed Roberts' 504 Sit-in Victory Rally Speech," Ollibean, last modified August 6, 2024, https://ollibean.org/ed/.
10. Martin Luther King Jr., "Letter from Birmingham Jail," *Atlantic Monthly* 212, no. 2 (August 1963), 78–88, available at https://www.csuchico.edu/iege/_assets/documents/susi-letter-from-birmingham-jail.pdf.
11. Steve Rose, "Dennis Billups: He Helped Lead a Long, Fiery Sit-in—and Changed Disabled Lives," *The Guardian*, September 16, 2021, https://www.theguardian.com/society/2021/sep/16/dennis-billups-he-helped-lead-a-long-fiery-sit-in-and-changed-disabled-lives.
12. "Our Story," OAK CLT, last modified March 20, 2023, https://oakclt.org/djcc/.
13. Leah Lakshmi Piepzna-Samarasinha, "Still Dreaming Wild Disability Justice Dreams at the End of the World," in *Disability Visibility: First-Person Stories from the Twenty-First Century*, ed. Alice Wong (Vintage Books, 2020), 256.
14. Amy Kenny, *My Body Is Not a Prayer Request: Disability Justice in the Church* (Brazos, 2022).
15. See, e.g., Shannon Dingle, "Resisting Ableism in the American Church," *Sojourners*, November 7, 2018, https://sojo.net/articles/resisting-ableism-american-church#main-content.
16. For more information on victims of filicide or other forms of caretaker violence, see the website for Disability Day of Mourning at https://disability-memorial.org/.
17. Leah Lakshmi Piepzna-Samarasinha, *Care Work: Dreaming Disability Justice* (Arsenal Pulp Press, 2021), audiobook.
18. Nancy Eiesland, *The Disabled God: Toward a Liberatory Theology of Disability* (Abingdon, 1994).

The Author

Tatum Tricarico is an activist, theologian, and director of Christian education at Wesley Memorial UMC in Charlottesville, Virginia. She has a master of divinity from Duke Divinity School and is a Disability Rights activist on Instagram (@blind_person_in_area), where she has curated a Disability cultural calendar.